INVESTIGA

- Gypsy or fortu...                                              ...nd.
  Find out why!

- Concerned about stress? The shape, condition, and quality
  of fingernails provide invaluable insights into tension,
  self-esteem issues, and physical health.

- A small percentage of people have fused head and heart
  lines called the simian line. What is its intriguing significance?

- Vertical lines found on the palm side of your fingers reveal
  possible exhaustion or tiredness. How?

- A long first finger (the index finger) can point you to
  certain career choices. What are they?

- Heartbreak or happiness? The heart line reveals emotional
  upheavals or strong, happy relationships . . . if you know
  the signs.

OPEN THE DOOR TO THE INNER SELF WITH . . .

**THE HAND BOOK**
**The Complete Guide to**
**Reading Hands**

# The Hand Book

## The Complete Guide to Reading Hands

NEAL CRISCUOLO

with

TONY CRISP

A DELL BOOK

Published by
Dell Publishing
a division of
Bantam Doubleday Dell Publishing Group, Inc.
1540 Broadway
New York, New York 10036

ISBN: 0-440-22140-4

First published in the United Kingdom by Optima in 1994

Printed in the United States of America

Published simultaneously in Canada

December 1995

10 9 8 7 6 5 4 3 2

OPM

*This book is dedicated with love to*
*Nicholas*
*Be good!*

# Contents

# Introduction

The information given in the following pages is aimed at providing an easily understandable guide to hand analysis. Blending traditional wisdom with modern scientific findings about the lines on the palm and the shape of the hand, this book gives uncomplicated ways of analyzing your own and other people's characters and vitality from the hand. To this we have added a unique feature: the intuitive look at the meaning of the lines. As far as we know, this has not been done before, and we believe it adds a great deal to the interesting information in the book.

If you have read other books on the hand, you may feel we have left out some of the details of hand analysis. This has been done purposely. The information left out has been replaced by a view of the hand that helps readers understand the areas of the hand so that they can fill in the details themselves. Many books on the hand give so much information that one has to learn it parrot fashion to gather it all in. Such books give a list of words of the qualities of an area. This book tries to foster a sense of the underlying processes of personality and body expressed in the hand. We hope this will lead to personal insight rather than just book learning. It should also lead to an ability to look at a hand and have an insight into it, rather than have forever to consult the reference book.

Hand analysis is not a mysterious practice. An understanding of its art can give an accurate and interesting insight into your own and other people's character and life. More than anything else, it is an excellent way to make friends and develop meaningful conversation. Virtually everybody enjoys hearing about himself or herself and having the luxury of talking openly of his or her own feelings, anxieties, and plans.

## Ancient Chinese Hand Analysis

The practice of hand analysis is thousands of years old. Used in ancient China as a means of psychological and health counseling, it later became a rather superstitious practice popularly known as palmistry. As such it was linked with fortune-telling and predicting a person's future. A more rational approach is taken in this book, and analysis is based on understanding the relevance of the palmar lines and the shape of the hand. The future may certainly be indicated by the configurations of lines and hand shape, but only because people's strengths and weaknesses predispose them to certain actions and relationships, and the results of these may occur many times.

## Gypsy Secrets of Hand Reading

Palmistry, or the art of the Gypsy fortune-teller, is not entirely ignored, however. The wonderful intuitive gift some Gypsies have, if understood, can be used by anyone who develops the skill through practice. Therefore a chapter on the use of intuitive hand analysis is included, rationally explaining some of the Gypsy secrets. This includes techniques for recognizing and developing one's own intuitive ability. It explains the various ways the human mind arrives at "intuitive" information. It gives a technique used by Gypsies to call on this gift suddenly when confronted by a complete stranger. We believe these features, like the intuitive information on the lines, are unique to this book and add to the literature on the subject even for those who have studied it for many years.

## Intuition Used in Researching the Book

The Gypsy technique described above can be used in many different ways. The intuitive response not only informs us about other people but can also synthesize our vast memory of information on any given subject. We have therefore used it to explore vague areas of hand analysis. For instance, writers commenting on the line called hepatica or health line frequently say that the traditional information is confusing and obscure. The intuitive information gained was very clear and definite. However, we have marked intuitive information as such to make sure the reader is aware of what is traditional and what is added by the authors through their intuitive research.

# 1

## The Hand

## A Short History of Hand Analysis

The practice of hand analysis goes back many thousands of years. No one can be sure when and where it was first practiced, but it probably originated in the East and from there spread throughout the rest of the world.

Many great ancient peoples, such as the Hebrews, Chaldeans, Tibetans, Babylonians, Egyptians, Greeks, Romans, and numerous others, have all given serious study to the science of hand analysis. Probably the oldest and definitely the most important studies took place in India and China. The ancient Indian Vedic religious texts, which date back almost two thousand years B.C., contain clear references to a practice of hand analysis developed at the time.

Later these teachings and traditions were taken by the Chinese and developed and modified by

Buddhism when it spread to China. Buddhism lends itself to the study of hand analysis because it is more of a philosophy of humankind and life than a religion and is free from many superstitions that other religions hold. Most important, Buddhism promotes a belief that humans create their own destinies. In Buddhist monasteries the knowledge was gathered by monks and passed down orally over generations. Methods and techniques were not divulged to outsiders, thus preventing bastardization by superstition and misunderstanding. The technique that developed was not a fortune-telling practice but rather a study of humankind developed over hundreds of years by cultures that in themselves were deeply perceptive. The teachings about the hand were based upon a sophisticated philosophy of life and a deep spiritual understanding of human beings.

There are not many places in the world today that you will not be able to find some form of hand analysis being practiced. Although methods do vary, it is likely they are all derivatives of those early Indian and Chinese methods, which have been modified to fit local religion, custom, and superstition. Today most of the respectable hand analysis techniques taught and practiced are based upon the very old Chinese methods even though few acknowledge this fact and some authors even claim that they or another contemporary have developed this amazing new and simple technique. Often the method and concept may be adapted for Western consumption, but it is clear that the most important influence in hand analysis today is the technique developed in China over twenty-five hundred years ago by the Buddhists. Modern books usually offer less comprehensive versions of these ancient teachings. But scientific studies *are* clarifying the connection among hand, brain, and personal history. They are also finding a concordance with much of the fundamental theories stated in the ancient teachings—principally, that through the hand much of the human condition can be diagnosed.

It is interesting that early European classifications and techniques not only were very crude and overcomplicated but lacked true understanding and now are being discarded or modified in favor of the older Chinese system, which is the original source of most traditional European techniques anyway. It's like returning to the source—rediscovering something taken and used but misunderstood and crudely interpreted, then finding the original methods again.

Apart from the defined information being uncovered by scientific investigation and through analysis of massive health and social data, I do not feel there have been any real advances made in hand analysis in recent times. Most of the techniques and concepts put forward today were dealt with by the Chinese many years ago. The area of advance today is that of dermatoglyphics—the study of the skin ridges on the palm—which is rapidly becoming a whole area of analysis of its own (see pages 267–77).

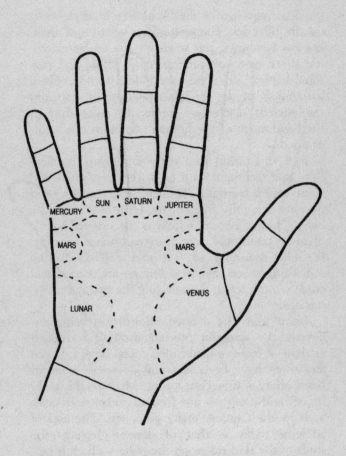

*Astrological Mounts*

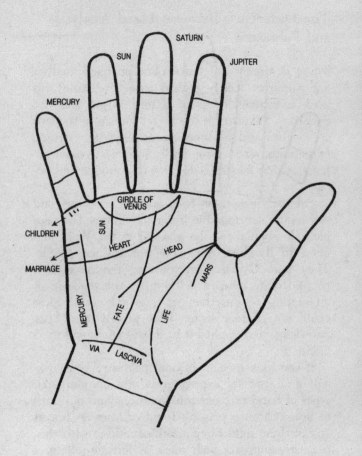

*Astrological Symbolism*

## The Difference Between Hand Analysis and Palmistry

There is a great difference between hand analysis and palmistry. It is helpful to define the two as this book is principally about hand analysis and not palmistry. Palmistry is the better known of the two approaches and is often associated with Gypsies, fairgrounds, and fortune-tellers. It is a romantic practice that falls into the area of mystique and occult.

Palmistry originates from ancient teachings and techniques developed in India and China. The people who popularized the practice in the West, and often in the East too, were not learned people. They were Gypsies, entertainers, and travelers—people trying to earn a living by the roadside or attempting to entertain or gain attention. Most could not read or write. They picked up a little knowledge and applied it in a very crude and fixed manner.

If you look in a traditional palmistry book, you will find that its explanations rely on particular types of hand or fixed configurations and positions of lines. Often a person's hand or lines do not fit any of these rigid categorizations. Along with this, palmistry supports such ideas as fortune-telling, a fixed and unalterable destiny, good and bad luck, curses, and other superstitions that are nonsense and potentially dangerous to the particular person. Any fear or respect that has been built around palmistry has been done by continuing to shroud the practice in mystery and by carefully wording readings so they make an impression. Often such hand reading arose out of quite rigid definitions of the lines or from clever, though untrained, intuitive perceptions of the person. Sometimes readings were clever generalized statements that could apply to anybody who was looking for assurance or was gullible—the sorts of phrases one finds in popular journalistic astrology.

Palmistry is therefore most likely the popular and generalized form of an older and more profound study of the hand. As such it took statements and made them into rigid rules to simplify and popularize. In doing so, it lost the overall view of the hand and the understanding of why the areas represented each aspect of human nature.

During the early stages of my interest in hands I read quite a few palmistry books, but I always found it difficult to remember the specific markings and their meanings because there was nothing linking all these pieces of information together. There was no underlying philosophy or understanding. Most important, there was no reason why certain lines meant certain things, just lots of unrelated pieces of information to remember. But relying on memory means that it is impossible to cope with markings that have not been remembered or dealt with.

Hand analysis approaches a reading from different fundamental attitudes. There is no good or bad luck, no thought of fixed destiny or fortune-telling, no rigidly fixed meanings for lines or hand types. It sees the hand as alive, part of our living body. The hand of each person is a unique expression of himself or herself. It is impossible to be specific or precise about markings, and it is impossible to give ex-

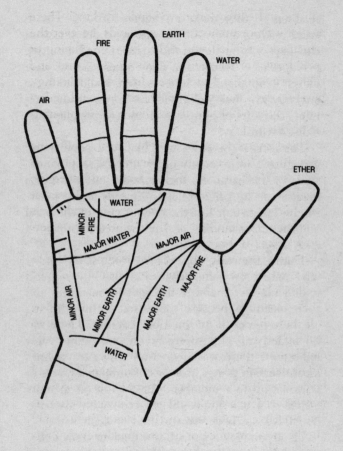

*Elemental Symbolism*

amples and explain every possible marking: There are an infinite number; no two hands are ever the same, not even left and right. But by grouping or sectioning the shape and areas of the hand and then providing a key to the lines and markings, hand analysis makes it possible to read and understand any hand—even those that contain unfamiliar markings.

Hand analysis can be described in the following way: It is the emotional, mental, and physical breakdown of the person's character and energies, using the hand as a map and indicator. It does not attempt to foretell the future but sees individuals as facing the random factors in their lives with personal strengths and weaknesses, skills or disabilities. Through the understanding of these personal factors, more enlightened choices and reactions can be made according to the circumstances.

The future is not given to us by a fortune-teller; it is ours already. If during a hand reading I were to make a prediction for the future, the person could decide consciously to make sure that my prediction did or did not come true, and in doing so, he would be creating his own future. Alternatively the person may be very suggestible and accept my prediction as true and live it out, but in this event there would also be an acceptance or decision made, even if unconsciously, and the future would still be created personally.

Hand analysis is about pointing out possible choices. It is an attempt to give a subjective view of character and personal energies and to point out individual responsibility for creating or achieving what you want. Without suggesting the lines have rigid meanings, hand analysis uses the lines as a framework to represent the major areas of human life, such as relationships and physical energy. From this a dialogue can arise with the person whose hand is being analyzed. Hand analysis recognizes that in any kind of counseling the counselor must be very careful in his or her approach and presentation of ideas and information to the person. An attempt is made to make a reading a two-way interaction, where you are helping people to reach a point of greater understanding of their problems and life situations.

It is in this area that palmistry fares particularly badly by restricting choice rather than encouraging it, providing a narrow view rather than an inclusive view. It therefore tends to take away personal responsibility rather than point out where it lies. What is needed is an overall understanding of the hands and what part the lines play in them. From this can arise a view of the hands that does not rely on fixed shapes or lines, and thus a more personal response to someone's hands can be given.

## Looking at Our Hands

Our hands are the servants of our mind. No sooner have we thought than our hands react immediately to the precise nature of our request. Mind and hands work in unison and harmony unlike any other part of the body. And we give less thought to the use of our hands than the use of ʌother part of our body; at times we must ʌ ʌte ʌn the use of our legs or arms, but the hands react almost without question, and thought is given only to the most precise and delicate of actions required. Not only can our hands perform an endless list of tasks, but they can express with great accuracy our feelings, thoughts, and needs as well. They can also touch and feel the world around and give information on the temperature, size, form, and movement of our environment.

We often use our hands to communicate when beckoning, waving, pointing, and gesticulating to add expression to the spoken word. Unlike spoken language, many of these gestures are understood universally.

Touch with another human can at times be almost electric, communicating love, passion, and tenderness. When we feel close to each other, we hold hands, and when we make love, hands can perform some of the most subtle but powerful acts of love. Conversely we can destroy with our hands, maim and kill. When we look around the world, we see that everything that is man-made has been constructed directly or indirectly with the use of our hands. The enormous variety of skilled activities hands can perform shows their power and how they are the tools with which we build our lives. Therefore a close examination of these tools may tell us about the quality of life we have created with them or what kind of world they have been used to build or are capable of building.

## Importance of the Thumb

The structure of the gorilla's hand is the closest to the human hand. When we examine the differences between a gorilla's hand and a human hand, we see that the fingers of an ape's hand do not have the degree of independent movement that the human fingers have and are capable only of grabbing and groping movements, the thumb being the greatest difference. The ape's thumb is very small in comparison to the human thumb, and although it has independent movement, it is very limited, and there is nothing like the large muscle structure that is built around the human thumb. The major difference, however, is that the thumb of the ape does not move in opposition to the fingers. This means apes can only grab objects in a folding motion and cannot delicately hold things between thumb and finger(s) as we do.

The thumb is the jewel in the crown of the human hand. Without the opposing thumb the human hand is nothing; it certainly would not have developed into the amazing tool we have now. What an opposing thumb means is that the movement of the thumb opposes the fingers, allowing us to touch the tips of each finger with our thumb. This highly developed movement of the thumb in particular is paramount in our performing some of the most basic and complex tasks with our hands. If you were to tape your thumb to the side of your hand, restricting all movement and use of the thumb, and then try to perform your everyday tasks, you would be surprised to find how difficult some of the most simple tasks become.

Whether it was the development of human intellect and consciousness that prompted the development of the human hand with its opposing thumb or whether the ability to use tools stimulated the growth of intelligence is not known. The process of refining the hand and intellect is still continuing today, though, and the hand still reflects the world of mind and spirit in human beings.

## The Palmar Lines

A common misconception is that the lines on the hand are crease lines. This is not true. In fact, the lines first develop on the surface of the palm while a child is still in the mother's womb. There are more nerve connections between the hand and the brain than any other part of the body. The lines on the palm are the result of electrical impulses from the brain to the hand along these nerve connections, and if something were to block or disturb this communication between the hand and the brain, the palmar lines would be dramatically altered.

An example of this is that the loss of the lines on the palms of the hands is a known warning of the onset of paralysis in the arms. This demonstrates the connection between the nervous system and the palmar lines.

The lines on the palm do not always remain the same. It is quite common for lines to appear or disappear, grow longer, or change in definition within a period of months or even weeks in some cases. Because of what was said about the nervous system/ brain link with the palm, such changes are likely to be linked with shifts in the personality and basic neurological functioning.

## The Character of Your Hands

People seldom study their own hands. Take a look at your hands. If you do, you may be surprised by what you see. Start by looking at the shape of the hand. Then look at the back of the hand and the fingers and their length. Now study your nails and thumb, and finish by examining your palm and the lines.

Where do the lines run? Are both hands similar or quite different? Are there lots of lines or just a few? If you haven't really looked at your own hands in detail before, you might feel you are looking at them for the first time. Something that I have done in the past was to look at my own hands in a mirror, a technique that seems to fool your brain into thinking that you are looking at someone else's hands. You are then able to get a much more subjective view of the shape and form of your own hands. Try this yourself, and while looking at your hands in this way, ask yourself what sort of person might these hands belong to. The character of your own hands becomes more obvious and pronounced as you notice the character of other people's hands.

## Take a Print of Your Hands

It is worth taking a print of both your palms so that if there are any changes in your palms, you can easily identify what they are. Also, more important, you are able to see for yourself that changes in the lines really do occur. When you have identified changes in the lines between a hand and an earlier print, you may like to take another print as a record of changing and developing lines. (See pages 219–21 for instructions on how to take a print.)

## Studying People's Hands

Although this book will give you a good basic understanding of hand analysis, if you wish to take this interest further, real knowledge and learning come from your own personal experience. After looking at your own hands, start looking at other people's. Notice how people's hands differ, how they are different from yours, and what feeling you get about them by just looking at the shapes and forms of their hands.

This is a good exercise to do while traveling to work in the morning on the train or bus or when you are shopping. Look at all the different types of hands around you, and without trying to think about them consciously, be aware of what feeling you have about each pair of hands you look at. Then look at the person. Notice how he is dressed, look at his face, observe his expression. Is he calm or agitated? What sort of person do you think he is?

Can you make a link between the person that you see and the type of hands he has? For example, a woman may look very beautiful, but her hands might give you a feeling of stress or coarseness.

Anyone reasonably serious about hand analysis needs to go through this exercise to build up his or her personal awareness of and relationship with the hand. The development of these are as important as learning the theory. The theory must be used together with your inner awareness for you to be able to give the best reading of a hand. Wherever I go and whomever I meet, it is now second nature for me to look at all the hands around me. There is always more to learn and recognize, and it is a continually developing process.

## Are the Past and Future Shown in Our Hands?

When we read hands, we must be aware that we are looking at a living part of the body and the hands are giving us information about a living being. If you have cut your hand at some time, the cut leaves a scar. The scar itself is not in the past, but it is an integral and important part of our living being now. What occurred previously has left its mark on your hand in the form of the scar, and this is a helpful way of thinking about how the past shows itself in the shape, lines, and marks on your hands.

What we have inherited genetically, what we have done with our bodies in terms of physical or mental work, and whether our hands have been heavily used or only held instruments that do not leave calluses all show in the shape, strength, and character of our hands. It is out of this that something of a person's past can be inferred from an examination of his or her hands. For instance, a woman recently showed me a large ridge crossing the nail of her big toes. This was due to a foot operation several weeks beforehand, and it was gradually moving toward the end of her toenail. With knowledge of the growth rate of her nails, the stress suffered could be dated. Marks on fingernails can be dated similarly, as can some marks on the palm.

For the future we work in a similar way when using hand analysis. We are not looking for any destiny in the hands but are considering the person as a living being who is always interacting with his environment while alive and thus creating reactions that we call the future. From the way we live now and from what we carry with us as inherited tendencies and health, we create our future. This is basic and understandable, just as when we smoke heavily in our youth, we realize there is a greater likelihood of premature death through lung cancer.

The interesting exercise is to work out from the attitudes, skills, and state of health the people have formed through their lives already lived what future they are creating for themselves and, from what shows in their hands, to help them to clarify it. In this way they can change direction where necessary.

I believe that we are all living only in the present. The past and future are concepts we carry with us. Every moment we are creating our future out of our present. This future is made continually out of how we feel, see, interact with, and understand the world around us at this moment. As external or internal influences change us, so our direction or future alters. From this point of view both the past and the future can be seen as an integral part of the present. Understanding them in this way makes it easier to interpret the areas of the hand that portray what people have already done with their lives and what may arise from this.

# 2

## Hand Classifications

### The Hand and Its Symbolism

The European tradition of palmistry used astrological symbols to explain and interpret the different areas and markings of the hand. For instance, the area at the base of the thumb is called the mount of Venus. The area opposite this—the percussion side of the palm—is named the mount of Lunar, and the areas of palm just beneath the fingers are given such names as the mount of Mercury, the mount of Jupiter, and so on. These names for the areas of the palm are fairly well known.

Fewer people are aware of the Chinese symbolism for the areas of the hand that are based on the elements of Fire, Earth, Air, Water, and Ether or Energy. Both the astrological symbols and the elements used in Chinese hand analysis are used to represent processes or characteristics seen working in nature. Ancient peoples were intelligent and expressed figuratively their observations of natural processes, like the modern use of symbols such as the chemical symbol for water, $H_2O$. The processes expressed by such symbols as the Earth element, or the Moon in astrology, were believed to be active at all levels of life—physical, mental, or spiritual. So the planet Mercury, the messenger, can represent the process of communication that occurs not only at a cellular biochemical level but also at a mental level, such as an awareness of unconscious content in processes like dreams, or communication through language and a sharing of self through art, songs, etc. and as an awareness of a personal connection with the universal processes of life.

The psychiatrist Carl Jung used the four elements of Earth, Air, Fire, and Water to represent four types of human personality: sensation, thinking, intuition, and feeling. These would represent people whose primary way of relating to the world would be through their sensory impressions under "sensation," their emotions under "feeling," their intellect under "thinking," and their inner intuitive impressions under "intuition." In hand analysis, areas of the palm are seen as an expression of the functions Jung describes. So the heart line would be studied to define the person's emotional response to life, and the head line for his thinking response. The areas of the palm represent functions in the body, in the mind, and within interpersonal relationships.

In the study of these areas of the hand both the astrological symbols and the Chinese elements will be used to give an understanding of how they are very closely matched. In areas where there is no astrological representation, reference will be made only to the Chinese elements. These elements are very easy to remember, and they apply to all areas of the palm. Even if you have already learned the astrological terms for the palm and prefer these, it is of value to know both approaches and understand the relationship between them. No matter which set of symbols you prefer to use, there is fortunately no conflict between the two schools of thought.

For myself, once I had understood the Chinese elements' system—from which the astrological was derived—I found I had a much better and fuller understanding of the astrological symbols in relation to the hand.

## Hand Shapes

There are four basic hand types, and these are symbolized by Earth, Fire, Air, and Water. There is no astrological equivalent to these categories.

Shape is the first classification that needs to be identified when you look at a hand. Shape is one part of the Chinese method of classification. The shape of the hand also gives an overall or general guide to the character of the person upon which all other qualities can be based and assessed. But we start our analysis with consideration of the palm shape. The palm itself is classified as being either square or rectangular.

- A square palm denotes a character that is emotionally balanced, rather practical, and providing stability.

- A rectangular palm denotes an emotional character—someone imaginative and seeking stability.

## Recognizing Differences Between Square and Rectangular Palms

Quite often you will be able to identify by sight a square or rectangular palm. If not, then you can take a ruler and measure the palm from top to bottom (wrist to fingers) and side to side (from the thumb side to the outer palm). In a square hand these two measurements will be very close or even identical, and in a rectangular palm the length from top to bottom will be greater than that measured from side to side and sometimes will vary quite considerably.

Obviously even with this guide there can still be some doubt with certain hands as to how the hand shape should be categorized. This will become easier with experience, but there are also other characteristics noted for each hand type that you may look to for help in confirming the category to which the hand belongs.

You may still come across hands that you are unable to classify; that is why I have explained the qualities of long or short fingers, square or rectangular palms independently so you may understand one of the qualities if you are unsure how to classify the other. It should give a better understanding of the qualities of the four hand shapes.

The fingers can be either long or short (see guide to finger length on pages 82–85 in the section on fingers), and the palm shape can be either square or rectangular, which gives the four basic hand shapes:

- Square palm/short fingers—Earth
- Square palm/long fingers—Air
- Long palm/short fingers—Fire
- Long palm/long fingers—Water

## Earth Hand

The Earth character is practical, conservative, and reliable. People with the Earth hand shape have a love of the countryside and all that is natural. Work is often linked to the earth in some way and preferably outdoors—e.g., building, cooking, gardening, farming. Earth people are not good communicators and find expression best in action or physically. When Earth people look for a partner, trust and security together with other very practical requirements are important factors; beauty and sophistication are not. Earth people are usually physically strong or well built and are seldom ill. The Earth hand has clear and deep lines, usually very few lines in addition to the major lines and thick or coarse skin.

## Air Hand

The Air character is intellectually inventive and unconventional. Air people are generally intelligent, are very good communicators, and enjoy intellectual stimulation. Work tends to be in areas

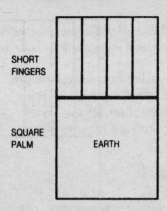

requiring technical or analytical ability, communication, or mental originality, such as computers, media, science, design (technical). Air people enjoy a sense of freedom; they are emotionally conservative and are rarely angry or upset. Unconventional in relationships, resisting or late in marrying, they may seek uncharted land in their choice of partner, personality and intelligence being more important than looks. Air people are usually quite thin and sometimes lack physical presence. They are sometimes prone to worry, and their health can suffer from this.

The Air hand is usually very large with thin, clear lines and dry, soft skin.

## Fire Hand

The Fire character is creative, energetic, and very active. Fire subjects are quite impulsive and naturally intuitive. They need activity and people

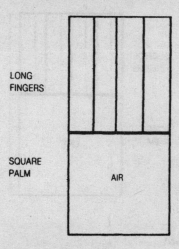

around them at all times to fuel their organizing abilities and need for attention. Work needs to be in areas where they can burn off their large amounts of energy. They prefer to be in a position of leadership and enjoy competition and the element of danger. Fire subjects are often respected and sometimes feared by their contemporaries. They enjoy influencing people and being in control of their environment. In relationships they can be impulsive, very emotional, and they look for partners who provide them with the excitement and emotional stimulation they enjoy. Fire people are usually fit and strong but have a tendency to excesses in eating, drinking, etc.

The Fire hand has strong, straight lines, usually many strong, clear lines in addition to the major lines and firm, warm hands.

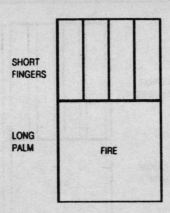

## Water Hand

The Water character is emotional, sensitive, and caring. Water people are very much influenced by others. It is important for them to be a part of groups, clubs, or social scenes. Work tends to be in areas where they are working closely with people and appreciated by others, such as social work, modeling, fashion, and design. Water people are very sensitive to their environment, and this can often be expressed creatively. Reliability and emotional security are important factors when they look for partners; because of their emotional vulnerability, attachment to the wrong partners can cause great emotional pain and uncertainty. Water people are usually slim and feminine in build. Their health can often suffer during times of emotional conflict.

The Water hand has fine lines that can be wavy or braided, usually many fine lines in addition to the major lines and damp, soft skin.

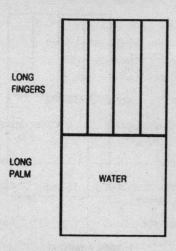

## Palmar Quadrants

The palm can be divided in two ways. First, we can draw a line horizontally through the middle of the palm dividing equally the upper and lower area. This shows us the upper area of the palm—that nearest the fingers—which represents "active awareness," and the lower area—that nearest the wrist—which represents "passive awareness."

Second, we can draw a line vertically from the middle finger down to the wrist, again dividing the palm equally. Now we can see the inner area—thumb side—of the palm, which represents "conscious activities" and the outer area—little finger side—which represents "unconscious activities."

Having made these divisions of the palm, we now have four clearly marked quadrants. Those four quadrants are known as:

- Passive/conscious—Earth
- Passive/unconscious—Water
- Active/unconscious—Air
- Active/conscious—Fire

**ACTIVE AWARENESS**

| ACTIVE UNCONSCIOUS AIR | ACTIVE CONSCIOUS FIRE |

**UNCONSCIOUS** ———————————— **CONSCIOUS**

| PASSIVE UNCONSCIOUS WATER | PASSIVE CONSCIOUS EARTH |

*PERCUSSION SIDE*　　　　　　　*THUMB SIDE*

**PASSIVE AWARENESS**

It is important to understand the qualities and influence that each quadrant has so that you have a deeper understanding of why the lines on the hand run along the routes they do. Understanding the significance of lines with uncommon configurations and interpreting minor lines that you have not seen before can really be done successfully only if you fully understand these four quadrants on the palm of the hand.

## Passive/Conscious Earth Quadrant

This quadrant of the palm, being that containing the ball of the thumb, represents the most basic and fundamental drives and urges within humans, such as physical energy, appetite, sexual drive, desire for life, strength of survival.

This area contains the instinctive energies of human beings, which, although very much an integral part of our conscious lives, are at a very primary or elementary level of our identities. When this is compared to the other quadrants of the palm, it is easy to see that it is the most muscular and powerful quadrant, supporting the thumb as it does and providing the thumb with independence and strength. The thumb describes the character of this quadrant. Because of its strength, it can act on the other parts of the hand in an independent manner and acts energetically upon them. The energy this quadrant provides is conscious and essentially supportive and represents personal identity at a fundamental level. Our sense of "I exist" rests upon these most basic and essential energies and drives.

## Intuitive Information on the Earth Quadrant

This area of the hand connects with the process in the body that takes up energy, directs it, and keeps things in place. It is the activity in us that takes hold of things such as food or thoughts and builds with them. In this it is rather like a seed planted in the soil. The roots of the seed take hold of the soil and take nutrients from it to build with.

It does not do this in a masculine controlling manner, but in a feminine receptive and self-relinquishing way. Although this process in us is not in control of the environment, it nevertheless uses it to survive. It is therefore receptive and expressive: receptive in that it receives from the environment, expressive because it builds or creates with what is

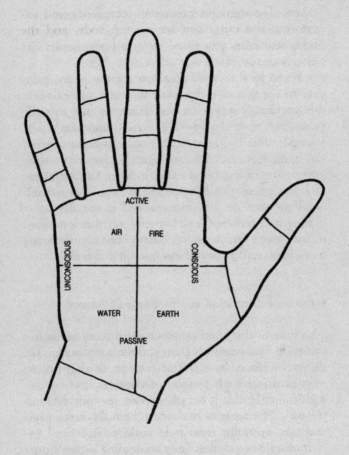

*Palmar Quadrants*

taken. Through this process of receptivity and expression the mind can act on the body, and the body responds, as a piano keyboard does under the fingers of the musician.

If you look at the hand, you see that some parts of the hand and some fingers aren't as active as others. Because this area holds the thumb, it is the most active and powerful part of the hand. The thumb itself is the most muscular and powerful of all the digits, and it also stands alone; it stands away from the others. This says something about the nature of this part of the hand. The strength and position of the thumb mean it can act upon other parts of the hand in an independent way. This ability to be independent and act upon the other parts of the hand or fingers has the characteristics of personal identity.

I sense the thumb and this area of the hand connect with the brain or represent self-awareness in a way that nothing else in the body does. It is out of the forces dealt with by this area that our identities emerge. The sense of "I am" has its roots here. This is why some early cultures used the thumbprint to represent their own unique identities.

Animals and lower life-forms do not have a sense of themselves as distinct from the rest of nature or as being separate from the urges and instincts moving them. They are moved by their own urges all the time and cannot decide to deny them. But humans are able to say, "I don't want to be something that's moved around. I want to be able to direct myself. I want to be able to move things. I want to take charge of my life."

This area connects with the inner processes and

attitudes in us out of which this power of identity rises, and the thumb more than anything represents that. The area of the ball of the thumb and the thumb itself, along with their strength, connect with the power of gaining control over oneself and life. So it is the power to receive from our environment and form or create our identity. The image of the seed with its emerging roots gives a good summary of this aspect of ourselves.

## Passive/Unconscious Water Quadrant

This quadrant represents a person's deep subconscious psyche, the inner nonphysical, nonmaterial world of creativity from which such things as dreams, imagination, intuition, art, music can be expressed. This tends to be the least developed area on most palms, and few lines originate here or are drawn across this quadrant, but I feel this is also the area of most potential within many of us.

This deep inner part of ourselves is an area that most of us, particularly in the West, are very unfamiliar with and have to a certain degree rejected. Therefore, when major lines are drawn into this quadrant of the palm, the subject is drawn away from the reason of the physical world into a world of creativity, dreams, imagination, but also at times uncertainty, irrationality, and even self-destruction.

This is the only quadrant on the palm that does not support any digits, and so it is quite clear that any expression from this quadrant into the physical world must be through one of the other three quadrants. It would be useful to imagine for a moment that we have a sixth digit that is supported by this quadrant but that has no form. Of course this digit has no effect in the physical world, but it represents our existence and awareness in the nonphysical world of thoughts, feelings, and fantasy or imagination.

The action this power of imagination and dreaming has in our life can be realized only if you consider what it would be like if you could live your life only day to day. If you lived through Monday and Tuesday and arrived at Wednesday, you would have to move on to Thursday and simply take what it offered. With imagination and dreaming, however, you can go back to Monday and relive or reconsider its events. In doing so, you could change them, see different possibilities in the events and relationships, and so alter what you might do during Thursday, Friday, and henceforward. So this realm, acting upon our conscious awareness, opens an infinite realm of possibility to us, if not of creativity in daily events certainly in the realm of art, music, drama, and social creativity.

### Intuitive Information on the Water Quadrant

This part of the human hand hasn't yet really been developed. There are possibilities here that human beings do not understand. Changes in personality and mental functioning could grow from this area when human beings have reached a certain point. There is a shadowy side of ourselves, a part that moves beneath our everyday awareness. For millions of years humans existed unconsciously, without self-awareness. In this state they gained an incredibly rich area of experience. In the development of self-awareness and a conscious ego, however, this massive and ancient collection of faculties was pushed into the shadows. But it is still powerful, it is huge, it contains much information. And because most of us deny its existence, it can become like something that is threatening, something that might even overpower, like a creature from the depths.

Thus people may relate to it in a negative way, become victims of it. They become casualties of life trying to develop another aspect of themselves. We see the results of this in all areas of human society, where apparently rational human beings kill one another in religious or political wars, driven by what can be seen as animal, unconscious territorial instincts or urges toward group identity and destruction of those outside the group.

Most of us touch this part of ourselves at some time in our lives, often positively. We are moved by intuitive urges toward safety; we have a sense of connection with a vaster awareness than we usually sense in our personalities or find powers of perception above the norm. These are brushes with this shadowy side of the self. Those of us who can relate to this massive area of experience, who can meet it and claim it as an aspect of ourselves, can open ourselves to another dimension of human ability. I see the shape of the hand changing if that is incorporated into society.

## Active/Unconscious Air Quadrant

This quadrant represents the subconscious persona of humanity, which yields itself to the physical world in the form of relationships. It links with our relationships with others, rational communication, emotional and creative expression and caring. This is the part of our character that we are less aware of and which is often expressed unconsciously. It is very giving and caring in its nature but, when given conscious direction, can be a source of very refined creativity and expression.

### Intuitive Information on the Air Quadrant

If human beings lost their ability to communicate, to live together socially and cooperate as they do, and they became insular, all the tremendous creativity that comes from cooperation would be lost. This is a factor that many people don't recognize. Everyday things, such as the clothes we wear, the cars we ride in, the entertainment we enjoy, the energy used in our houses and businesses all arise from our being able to work cooperatively.

Our ability to cooperate and to communicate within that cooperation is represented in this area of the palm. Although this area has its roots in sexuality, reproduction, love, and those basic drives that come from our subconscious, it has developed far beyond that and has been refined into areas of incredible sharing of information and cooperative skill.

Although this area of the hand appears less functional physically than some other parts, it is actually an amazingly well-designed tool. This area connects with human love—not romantic love but something else. Human beings have to exist together in a way that is quite unusual apart from some insects. Among mammals there are few that work together in quite the way that human beings do, and this area of the hand has something to do with this. It is concerned with relatedness, the area of learning social relationships, and this of course has its beginnings in our part of the evolutionary tree with the apes. But we have refined it to an extraordinary degree, and in doing so, we have become incredibly creative and incredibly communicative. This area represents this relatedness and the creativity and communicativeness that are a part of it. This is why the astrological system puts Mercury in this area.

Although this area connects with the unconscious drives to survive and reproduce, these drives have been extended and refined in this area of the human psyche. My intuitive look at this aspect of the hand tells me that the physical body itself has adapted to this growing relatedness that human beings have, and this area of the hand particularly has to do with the changes that have gone on. This part of the hand has altered because human beings have had to leave certain things behind in learning to relate to one another; otherwise they couldn't have cooperated in the way they do. Thus the personal struggle for survival has given way to a more communal struggle. They are still learning, so they have not fully left those things behind. This part of the hand is a lot more open and expanded because of this communal ability.

So this quadrant is a link with something bigger than ourselves. It is where our personal drives give way through love for others, for society, and therefore for a greater whole.


## Active/Conscious Fire Quadrant

This quadrant represents the human ego, one's sense of self, self-esteem, and confidence as projected to the outside world. This area of ourselves contains the energies that drive us forward to create our presence in the world, such as our ambition and ability to utilize the environment to our advantage. Through these drives we manifest the aspects of ourselves known to others through our actions, speech, and relationships. If these energies are well expressed, personal direction and decisiveness will be strong, while challenges and ambitions can be taken on very dynamically. This is the part of our character that we are most aware of because it is how we consciously place ourselves within society and interact socially as individuals.

This area of the hand is much more personal than all the others in that each of us develops different abilities and levels of skill. Even with skills that are common to us all, such as writing, there is a very particular way of writing for each person. So although the Earth quadrant represents the personal "I exist," this quadrant is about "who I am that exists"—our personal characteristics, personal skills, personal refinement or coarseness.

Lines, and the characteristics they display, that are influenced by or run through this quadrant take on the personal image and drive qualities of this sector. This strongly affects how people project themselves into society.

### Intuitive Information on the Fire Quadrant

This area has such a lot of meaning in it that it is difficult to sort out what's relevant. A starting point might be that if a person lost the hand he used most, he would feel as if a whole area of his life had been lost. For instance, his writing, manipulative skill, and capacity to use lots of personal abilities would be lost. These skills are often closely linked with this area of the hand.

This quadrant of the hand and the quadrant connected with the thumb are so interlinked in their action it can be difficult to define them separately. So by thinking of losing the hand, we can clarify what part the Fire quadrant plays in our life. Everything from writing, painting, and needlework to communication and reaching out to touch somebody involves this area of the hand and the first two fingers particularly.

Thinking about the first and second fingers in relation to this sector helps define the meaning of this quadrant. We use these fingers to move things about, to manipulate things in the world. Through them we express what skill or lack of skill or strength or quality we bring to dealing with all the things that we try to control or change or create in the world. So the area relates to our will, but it isn't the same as the thumb.

Looking at this area of the hand from the point of view of hand analysis, we see the amount of personal self-confidence or personal value that a person has. It shows the image we have of ourselves or how we feel others see us. This can be seen in the way the person uses this part of the hand and also how well developed it is, its refinement and its relationship to the thumb. If we consider what is going on between the thumb area and this area, we can tell a person an enormous amount about himself that is very helpful practically. For instance, if you note how people hold pens or pencils when writing, you will notice many different styles. With some people the intense stress obvious in their grasp of the pen indicates the difficulties they have in the relationship between their self-confidence and self-expression. Other people hold pens lightly and easily, manipulating them with great artistry.

Another example can be seen in the second fingers of people who are not extroverting themselves easily. This finger doesn't come into play so much in their lives; it is not so strong; it is not so mobile; it may not have the mounds underneath it developed so fully. This suggests that such people haven't allowed themselves to extend their inner lives. The area links with their external abilities, but the second finger has more to do with them, their subjective inner lives that they express in relationship with the world. For some people that part of them hasn't been developed. They haven't developed a philosophy of life or a clear image of themselves. They are not clear about what they can contribute to the world. In effect they are still being moved around by events and urges from the unconscious. So the second finger is significant because helping a person define how he can find what he can contribute and how to express it is very important. It gives a person poise and a sense of sureness in his relationships with other people.

Where the muscular connection among the second finger, the palm, and the thumb is underdeveloped, it suggests these people have not matured their ability to reason or grasp situations in life rationally. This will make it more difficult for them to actualize themselves. They have not clarified their motivations, and so they are haphazard in the world. One might say their personalities have not yet unfolded fully. But where the musculature between the first two fingers and the thumb is well formed, then it suggests these people have developed qualities that have placed them firmly in the world. It is almost as if they had built electrical circuits. They have wired themselves into the world and made connections—not just one or two but a whole series of connections with activities and other people. This will show in the work they do, in their social lives, in being socially recognized and respected by other people.

## The Natural Hand Position

When looking at people's hands, I ask them to open their hands naturally, in the way that feels easy to them. In opening their hands they should let their fingers fall into their natural positions.

## Close-Held Fingers

Fingers will sometimes spread outward; sometimes they will be bunched together. There are lots of formations that the fingers might fall into naturally, and this can tell us something about a person's character also. If the person holds the fingers closed with no spaces between them, this shows him to be somewhat introverted. The closeness also suggests that all the qualities of the fingers are very much blended together, not independent of one another and without independent expression.

I tend to find that people with closed fingers often have quite stiff fingers that resist if I try to move them. These people are less adventurous, or they are held by convention. It is almost as if, with their fingers held together like that, there were parts of themselves they do not want to expose or express. It is a bit like being afraid of being seen without any clothes on. These people are not particularly original in expression and will follow in already trodden paths. There is a certain amount of rigidity in the way they express themselves too.

## Open-Held Fingers

When there are spaces between the fingers, the qualities of each of the fingers remain independent. If people's fingers are very widely spaced, it means they are generally extroverted. They often have very open and original expressions and are much more prepared to change and are less rigid in their outlooks. The very widely spaced fingers are not impacting and not drawing from one another.

## Leaning Fingers

Quite often fingers may bend toward another finger. This shows that the finger bending toward another —or the qualities represented by that finger—is expressing itself through the qualities of the finger that it is pointing toward. It must be read as growing toward the qualities of the finger it is pointing to.

There is a difference between fingers growing "toward" another digit and those that lean "on" another finger. If fingers are leaning on another finger, not growing toward it, they are dependent or being supported by the quality of the finger they are leaning on. It is important again to remark on the quality of the fingers. Look at the fingers, how straight they are, how solid. If you think of energy being channeled or directed through that finger, what does that finger tell you? It is when you really look at fingers and when you really consider what you can see, whether the fingers are strong, are straight, or have that certain power about them, that you begin to see the strengths and weaknesses of the person before you. Perhaps a finger might be slightly bent or may not be quite so thick or a little spindly or in some way underdeveloped. All these characteristics can tell you the strengths within the person. You may see strengths in one finger and maybe weaknesses in another.

In hand analysis we are looking for those strengths and weaknesses. There is a line that is normal, and we are looking for qualities above and below that line. It is a bit like a doctor looking for symptoms, causes, and effects. You are not looking for the norm particularly, you are looking for those things that can give you an insight into who this person is, and so you are looking for the anomalies or irregularities within the hand that can give an insight into the person's character. When I am holding a person's hands and doing a reading, I quite often like to see how much flexibility there is in the hand and the fingers. I try to move the fingers slightly, and sometimes there is a lot of tension in the hand. If I try to fold the fingers inward, sometimes there is a lot of resistance to that movement. Others people's hands can be very supple or even extremely supple or limp, and all this is extra information. Where the fingers are very difficult to move and there is a lot of resistance in the hand, this can give an indication of the tension the subject is carrying and how uptight the person is. When the hand is very supple but firm, you can see the relaxed nature and strength of the person. If the hand is limp and lacking strength, this also gives you an indication as to the character of the person.

# Intuitive Information About Reading a Hand

When I am analyzing a hand, my unconscious suggests the Fire quadrant is the area to look at first and to talk to the subjects about. This is the area they fully understand. They are not so conscious of the other parts of themselves, and it is from here one can help them find their way into the areas of which they are not so aware. A good analytical process would be to understand the relationship of the Fire quadrant with the other three quadrants. The relationship among the quadrants needs to be really looked at, not just the quadrants by themselves. How they relate to one another is of immense importance, especially to the person you are talking to.

What they can observe of themselves, what they are aware of as being their character, and how this relates to the different aspects of themselves in the less conscious areas of the other quadrants give them the power to improve the quality of their lives.

If you started by looking at the mount of Lunar, often the person would not identify with what you say. But if, for example, you take the relatedness of the Fire quadrant to the mount of Lunar/Water quadrant, the person can observe how he is expressing himself externally, and what he observes is what actually happens in the world. If some awareness of the underlying attitudes and fears that lead to certain actions can be gained, a great change can occur in his life.

Many people's lives are geared around what they can observe happening externally. If they can begin to understand the connection between what they do and the other forces of emotion and drives within them, they might now say, "Well, I didn't do too well there," or "I didn't quite satisfy myself with that." Knowing how urges from aspects of themselves other than their conscious egos can either add to or detract from the quality of their lives will enable them to guide their lives in a more satisfying way. So in that sense helping people understand the structure of other parts of their nature can help them produce a different quality of action in the world.

## Left and Right Hands

When we conduct a hand analysis, both the left and right hands must always be taken into consideration. Each hand represents quite distinct areas of our characters. Therefore the left and right hands must be fully understood in their importance and meaning to be able to interpret correctly and balance one hand against the other. The next chapter looks in detail at the significance of the left and right hands.

# 3

# Left and Right Hand

The story of left and right takes us back to prehistoric times, in fact to the Paleolithic period, when a left-hand dominance was found to exist in these early human beings. The evidence for this comes from careful studies of stone tools of the time and, more interestingly, the cave paintings. These were found to be right-profiled drawings, leading most prehistorians to believe these paintings could have been done only by left-handed humans.

Studies of tools used during the Neolithic period and the later Stone Age show clearly a period of both left- and right-handedness. The first signs of right-hand dominance appear during the Bronze Age with the sickle, a tool that was made for the right hand only. So from this brief history of "handedness" you can see the possibility that left-handedness developed into ambidexterity, which then gradually gave way to the right-hand dominance.

There is a theory that our right-handedness came about from the realization that the heart is on the left side and therefore should be protected. While shielding this vulnerable left side, the right hand was free to throw stones and sticks. So it could be said that right-handedness grew out of greater awareness of self and self-preservation as well as out of a more aggressive human nature.

For many thousands of years humans looked upon the left side with hate and fear because it signified weakness and vulnerability. It is the side that they must take so much care to protect, whereas the right hand is associated with dominance, survival, and aggression. It seems that to become the dominant species that we are today, humans not only physically rejected their left side but also psychologically rejected all those parts of themselves symbolized by the left side.

Even in this century children who had an inclination toward left-handedness were forced to write with the right hand. In some religious schools the children were told the left hand belonged to the devil and must never be used. This illustrates the immense social pressure toward conformity existent in connection with which hand was dominant.

## Left and Right in Language

Looking at the words "left" and "right," we see that "left" by its own definition says that it is the side that has been left, put to one side, or is the remaining side. When I think about the left, I get the feeling that it really is the side that was left behind, it is the physical and psychological side which we chose not to develop, it is part of our past that we still carry today somewhat awkwardly and with just as much symbolism as ever.

In many languages you will find a negative meaning that is so often applied to the left side. In the Italian language the word for "left" is *sinistro*, which gives a clear indication of the origin of the word, connecting as it does with the English word "sinister," which is defined as "connected with evil, or looking villainous." In French the word is *gauche*, meaning "lacking in ease or grace."

Even the sayings that we use illustrate how the left is used as a definition for wrong or useless. For example, "He has two left feet" means awkwardness or clumsiness; "Marry with the left hand" means marriage to a person of higher rank but with no claim to possessions or title. Superstition of previous centuries suggested the devil sits on our left side, and that is why we throw salt over our left shoulders. In many other cultures, evil spirits are believed to sit on the left side. We never shake hands with the left hand, and in some Eastern cultures to give or accept anything with the left hand is considered wrong or offensive.

In contrast, the word "right" is associated with everything that is good, honest, and straight. We say things such as "Do the right thing," "a righteous person," "right-of-way," "in his right mind," and "right as rain." Right is the chosen side and by its own definition is everything that is not wrong. It is the acceptable, good, and, more important, powerful side. Right is associated in all languages with straightness, justice, law, and truth. In Italian the word for "right" is *destro*, and in French it is *droit*. The English word "dexterity" comes from the French *dextérité* and the Latin *dexteritas*. Their meaning is "right-handedness." All these words give us the same definition of the right side as being capable and correct.

## The Right Brain/Left Brain Influence

If the theories concerning the influence the left and right sides of the brain have upon human behavior are correct, this may be a factor in right- and left-handedness. The left lobe of the brain, for instance, is almost always larger than the right lobe. Considering that the left lobe controls the behavior of the right side of the body, and the right lobe controls the left side, there are direct connections between the brain lobes and the hands. Differences other than size also occur between the lobes. The left lobe contains many short neural fibers that provide rich interconnections within limited areas of the hemisphere. The right lobe contains many long neural fibers that connect widely separate areas.

The difference between what the lobes do in terms of our experience and behavior has been defined because of a form of treatment given to a few sufferers of an acute form of epilepsy. Usually there is a connecting bridge of nerve fibers, some two hundred million of them, called the corpus callosum. This bridge is severed in the epilepsy patients, forcing the lobes of the brain to act independently. From this it was discovered that:

- The left hemisphere of the brain controls the right side of the body, speech, reasoning, a sense of past and future.
- The right side of the brain controls the left side of the body, the spatial sense, intuition, awareness of gestalts, arriving at meaning through putting together many small bits of information, feelings, the present.

If a person with a split brain closes the left eye, she can read because the right eye sends impressions to the left lobe, which deals with language. But if the right eye is closed, she cannot read because the right brain does not deal with this skill.

The rational, active left side of the brain controls the right hand. So there may be a link between right-handedness and the left brain lobe, as this lobe/hand link produces a more controlling, active link with the world. The right lobe/left hand link would deal more with emotions, intuition, spatial sense and artistry, or a holistic view or connection with the world.

## Left and Right in Hand Analysis

Left and right is quite an extensive subject in itself, and we have only briefly touched on it, but you can see clearly how handedness is deeply rooted in our bodies, society, and culture and that you need only look around you to gain a greater understanding of left and right and the dominance of the right.

In hand analysis we refer to active and passive hands. For a right-handed person the right hand is the active hand and the left the passive hand, and in a left-handed person the left is active and the right passive. So it is important when making a reading of hands to establish whether the subject is right- or left-handed and not to assume that he or she is right-handed. There are interpretations of left-handedness itself that we will deal with shortly, but first we will look at active and passive hands.

Between the active and passive hands what we are looking for are the differences more than the similarities. If they were both exactly the same, you could probably get away with reading one, but if they are dramatically different, then there is obviously a division or even a conflict between the person's inner and outer world or his inner and outer expression. Some people's active and passive hands are very different while others are quite similar. Generally you will find some differences between active and passive, however minor.

It is an interesting subject in itself to look at the differences between passive and active hands. If I am looking for things that have happened in the past, in the person's childhood, I would generally look on the active hand first because that gives me a clearer indication of the effect of that past. It shows the results of his life until today. It is generally clearly marked on the active hand. If this is not the case, but there are signs of strong events on the passive hand, then it is a more hidden, underlying kind of result. So it's a balance between the passive hand and the active hand.

Remember when you are comparing active and passive hands that there can be all sorts of differences to identify. It would be easy just to look for differences in the lines of the palm, but you will find that all areas of the hand can show differences. Therefore a close examination of both hands must be carried out. It is worth paying close attention to lengths of the fingers, direction and shape of fingers, size and build of the thumb. All of these can show differences between the two hands.

If there is little difference between the active and the passive, it suggests there is more balance between the person's deep underlying character and what he is on the social level, on the outgoing level. If there are deep differences, you can see how far somebody has traveled and moved on from what he gained from his family and cultural heritage and what he has become through personal effort. Such differences show the effort the person has made to become more positive or to overcome difficult areas in concentration or physical health. This is particularly evident in the body. It is amazing that if somebody has been very physically fit in the earlier years of life, the ball of his thumb in the passive hand is very large, but it is smaller in their active hand because the person is no longer sustaining its fitness. This can also apply the other way around. The passive hand may be weaker and the active larger, showing how such people have actually built themselves up over the last few months or the last year or two.

### Active Hand

This hand represents the conscious self, the individual, our self-determination, the character that we are most familiar with and that is visible to the outside world, attitudes and directions that we are aware of or have purposefully made. It represents the present in that the qualities in this hand are being realized and exploited actively within life at present. The active hand is a good indication of the conscious and immediate well-being of the subject. Problems or disturbances within this hand can be said to have affected the person's life visibly and consciously. Past marked events on this hand will still carry some active effect in the present. All characteristics interpreted from this hand must be thought of as dominant and active within the person's conscious life.

### Passive Hand

This hand represents the unconscious self, hereditary and family characteristics, qualities that we are usually unaware of that have fundamental influences on our lives. It is the character that we are least familiar with and possibly parts of our character that we wish to keep concealed or repressed. The passive hand does not really represent the past. Past events can be seen on both hands, but I feel the passive hand can contain a person's potential. It shows qualities that are held by the person that, if desired, could be developed and exploited. In this case they may be eventually seen in the active hand.

The passive hand indicates the fundamental and more long-term well-being of the person. Problems, disturbances, and past events marked in this hand can be said to have had a greater fundamental effect on the person, but unless also marked on the active hand, the effects have been concealed or repressed and therefore have no conscious effect on active life. All characteristics in this hand must be interpreted as secondary and passive within the person's life.

The passive hand shows influence of our family background and culture. It shows the potential, the subconscious aspects of our character that are the foundations upon which our exterior expressions rest. So its shape and lines portray all those passive parts of ourselves that are our potential.

If we think of a person like a house, while the visible surface part of the house may go through many changes during its life, being painted different colors and having extensions added, etc., the foundations are very seldom changed. Likewise, the marks on the passive hand do not change much, as they are our foundations. There are some things in the passive hand that can develop, though; it depends upon the person's ability to remodel himself. Many people look upon their past as buried and best forgotten. Others extract what value they can from it and polish any treasures found within themselves from it. Such strengths in the character of a person would determine his ability to change the passive hand.

The lines and shape of the active hand seem to

react and change much more than those on the passive hand. So the active hand is more reactive, but the passive hand is more conservative or subdued. Because of this, the lines on the active hand show a lot more of what is going on and changing in the person's life, and you can read a lot more in it. Because the passive hand deals with all the inherited patterns of behavior we get from our culture and family and the deeply habitual parts of our personality, it is more difficult to change and deal with these aspects of our lives than those found in the active hand.

If, for example, you can see there is a lot more tension in the passive hand than in the active hand, this suggests there is a lot more underlying or inhibited tension. That might be more difficult for the person to change because it is habitual and people are less familiar with that side of themselves because it is largely unconscious.

## Comparing Left and Right

When observing the left and right hands, you will tend to see a correlation between the two even if the hands vary considerably in their markings. All such differences should be noted; then the two hands can be balanced against each other to see how they correspond to each other. The differences between left and right are found not just in the lines but also in the fingers, thumb, nails, and general shape and size of all areas of the hand. If there is uncertainty over whether a person is right- or left-handed, the best rule is to find out which hand he uses to sign his name, and you can be safe to assume that that hand is the dominant or active hand.

One interesting point to mention is the fact that Gypsy or fortune-telling palmists read only the left hands of their clients. Because they believe that people cannot change their own destinies, the readers actually ignore the right hand, and in doing so, they are rejecting the person's self-determination, rejecting his ability to control and master his environment and instead accepting and interpreting only the passive, hereditary, and unconscious influences that are represented in the left hand.

## Right-handedness

I cannot see a need to give an interpretation of right-handedness in a person because the vast majority of people are right-handed, and therefore the qualities apply near enough to everyone. Nevertheless we should understand that the right-handed characteristics show that the person is active and masculine in nature and his expression is through logic and reason.

## Left-handedness

Left-handedness can be found in only 3 percent of the world's population—a clear indication of the dominance of right-handedness. Left-handedness can be traced far back into humanity's past, and as already explained, it is an element within human beings that has been pushed to one side, discarded, but it has not been lost completely. Today "left" preference still survives within a small minority of people.

The superstitions and fears from the past regarding left-handedness should not be encouraged today. Left-handed people are neither sinister nor stupid. Children who show a left-hand preference should certainly not be forced to use the right. This is known to cause much harm. The left-handed characteristics are simply that the person is passive and feminine in nature, and his expression is emotional and imaginative.

## Left and Right Through the Eye of Intuition

Something about hand differences that often is not mentioned is that it has to do with the symmetry between the left and the right. This goes right through the body—the hands, the nose, the eyes, the ears. In nature you find this symmetry going on everywhere in things like leaves, beans, and anything that has two lobes, two sides.

This connection with hand analysis is quite an important consideration in that the way the body forms involves a branching-like action from a center. In our bodies that starts with two cellular lobes that fold around and produce the two sides of the body. The left hand in the physical sense is no less, no more than the right hand. But in what has happened in our culture there has been a dominance, an evolution toward right-handedness.

If you take the paws of a dog, there is no dominance. With human beings we have a side that predominates. So even at the muscular level there is more power in the dominant side of the body, and the symmetry is disturbed. By "disturbed" I mean changing the flow of something in such a way that it causes the shift in symmetry. From this the separation between left and right occurs, and the changes in structure—physical structure, size, shape, but also the lines on the hands—occur. This disturbance took a long time in human culture to reach the point it has today, and the changes, the differences are very pronounced. The roots of the differences are linked with the whole emergence of human culture and human personality.

So in the beginning there was symmetry, and out of this disturbance arises. Then there is a shaping. In the early stages of their development human beings began to feel themselves cut off from nature. Because of their emerging self-awareness, they felt themselves isolated, no longer a part of the normal flow of things. They realized they could make decisions, and this ability to make a personal decision instead of being moved by forces of nature had a tremendous impact on human beings. This occurs with growing children as they come to the realization of "I"—I can, I won't, I will, I won't go to the toilet, I want to go to the toilet.

Out of this the left and right difference of symmetry began to arise. In this case the left represented what had dominated until the emergence of will. What had dominated the human being then still influences us unconsciously now, but what acted upon humans unchecked can now be denied by our will. It is all the cultural influence, the physiological influence, the family influence that play upon us unconsciously, the way the light plays upon a plant. Those influences play upon the forming of the human personality, but the human personality can react to them in various ways, possibly denying them entirely, in which case you might have a very weak left hand compared to the right. The symmetry could be very definitely interfered with in that case. Or you might make an ally of those influences and take them and develop them. In this case the symmetry isn't broken, it isn't oppressed, but because of the development, there is a complementary change, a difference.

In regard to hand analysis the hand that doesn't predominate carries in it signs of the formative factors of the human personality. The factors that give our personality its foundations and its shell can be taken away or denied only with great risk. So disturbances or signs of weakness in the left or nondominant hand show a lack of power underlying the person.

Unless people worked upon themselves very deeply, they wouldn't eradicate those signs of weaknesses; they would stay in the hand. It would have to be a very thorough psychological working to change those signs. It would not be like redecorating one's house and making the interior and the furniture very different. It would be akin to actually pulling the walls down and rebuilding bits.

A woman tends to allow more of the influences

of her less predominant side into her personality. So there is not often that marked difference as in the male. Looking at a woman's nondominant hand, you might see in it features that are really almost predominant, especially in her emotional life. More frequently her personality is based upon traditions because of her connection with her feelings and intuition. A man's nondominant hand would show his background, where he has come from, what his beginnings were. He may have cut himself off from them, he may have attempted to change them, developed them, or he may have deserted them in a greater way than a woman would have.

I believe there was a period in human evolution when a critical point was reached and a new direction was taken. Up until that time human beings felt themselves to be alone in some way, to be quite different from the other animals, and out of this they had developed a feeling of uniqueness. They could see their form was similar to that of the animals, but they felt that something had happened to them, that something had come into them to make them special, almost like a spirit that entered them and changed them. They felt chosen, as if by a great godlike being. It is not that they thought they were equal to the god but that they thought they were worthy of the god.

Out of this sense of specialness they began to have a feeling of dominance in a way they had not experienced before. They felt righteous or good in the eyes of their imagined god. This produced such a change, and they felt that they had a right to the world, even the right to kill each other. Because we are descended from them—we inherit that—we are the inheritors of what they did.

As a consequence, human beings made a judgment about natural impulse and spontaneous love. The judgment was that such parts of human nature were evil. For instance, natural sexuality is still taboo today. It is acceptable if it is out of public view, but punished socially if made obvious or in public figures. And it was the shunning or pushing away of what had been such a large part of these early humans' lives, in their urges and feelings, that brought about the break between left and right. From this period of human history we are left the feeling that there are parts of ourselves we have to be sneaky about and there is something to be shunned in us.

Left-handedness in our time often occurs in people who feel there is something in their births or their lives that makes them believe they are not a part of the social mainstream. Perhaps it runs in the family, but it is almost as if it were their karma to try to reclaim something that has been destroyed, to experience themselves in the left hand. It is like a lesson they are learning, a lesson in meeting the feelings of being different. It is rather a difficult lesson for some people to be left-handed, to feel different, odd, to feel that they are not the predominant one. If they can accept past lives, the lesson they are learning is the lack of dominance—quite a profound thing to learn.

# 4

## The Thumb

The most conspicuous evolutionary development in the hand is shown by the growth of the thumb. Isaac Newton once remarked that in the absence of any other evidence the thumb alone would convince him of God's existence, and the French writer Malcolm Czar made the astute comment that fingers must be educated, but the thumb is born knowing.

The thumb deserves a place of honor. It symbolizes the greatest achievement of the species. Human hands differ from animal hands essentially in the separation of the thumb from the four fingers. Any irregularity of the thumb is of greater significance than the shape, length, or irregularity in any other feature of the hand. Therefore in hand analysis it is important to look at the thumb very closely and be aware of its proportion in relation to the four fingers and the palm.

In most cultures the thumb has represented personal power. Some tribal people, if they were meeting on a peaceful basis, would hold their thumbs tucked within their fingers to show they were holding back their dominance. In ancient China the thumbprint was often used as a personal signature on documents or on the base of pottery. The thumb was also used in ancient times as a symbol of power and fertility. In some countries in the past slaves had their thumbs cut off to symbolize the loss of power over their own egos.

When babies are first born, their thumbs are clenched within their fingers and are submissive. This shows that the babies have not yet used their thumbs to influence their environment. As they grow and explore their environment, the thumb is released and becomes proud. When the thumb is held within the palm in an adult, it is a sign of repression of one's own ego, an expression of the holding back of oneself or of a surrendering to outside forces. I have often noted the thumb being held in this position by people who are feeling anxious or overwhelmed by life or a situation.

The thumb is the single most powerful digit on the hand. It is supported by a large amount of muscle tissue at the base; it is the only digit that has two phalanges (a section of bone in the finger or thumb; the fingers have three) and has the greatest amount of mobility and independence. The thumb holds a position of great power on the hand, and without it the hand would be virtually useless. The separation and development of the thumb are what sets a human being's hand apart from similar structures in all other animals.

Take a close look at your own thumb. Look at its

form and position and how it stands proudly upon the hand. Nevertheless the thumb is still basically passive and supportive in its role; we do not reach or point with our thumbs, and we do not touch and feel with our thumbs. When we write or paint, the thumb does not manipulate or direct; rather it supports. So looking at the basic physical role of the thumb is a good introduction to the interpretation of the thumb in hand analysis. Use of the thumb in idioms such as "thumbs up," "thumbs down," and "being under the thumb" also gives us a clue to the power but also the quality of power of this digit that is being communicated in those well-known phrases.

Because the thumb is connected with how we express ourselves personally, it links with what Carl Jung called individuation. Individuation means to become uniquely ourselves. During life we all develop certain traits. At first we can be thought of as being like a rock in its natural state. Gradually, however, marks or carvings are left on the rock by how we educate ourselves and the efforts we make to develop certain mannerisms and skills. People individuate. They become more refined, characterized, different from anything or anyone else. In doing so, we become more distinct, less like anyone else, removed from nature in a way.

That is a good word for the thumb: distinctness. The thumb itself is distinct from the fingers and from the hand.

# Interpreting the Significance of the Thumb

The only true way to describe the thumb with regard to its position on the hand is as the rudder that guides the ship. The thumb is an indication of how assertive people are, whether they are able to express themselves in satisfying ways during their lives, and how capable they are of influencing and mastering the environment around them. There are many qualities that can be read from the hand, but we must be aware of the great influence the interpretation of the thumb exerts on these qualities. The thumb shows or determines how people can assert and realize their innate qualities during their lives. In fact, the thumb is considered with such high regard that when reading the hand, some palmists in India take their readings solely from their observations of the thumb.

When we begin our interpretation of the thumb, we first look at its form. This applies to all areas of the hand but in particular, I feel, to the thumb. When looking at the form of the thumb, notice what impression it gives you. Is it pleasing? What are the proportions with regard to the rest of the hand? This first look at the form of the thumb as a whole will give a good general image of the type of thumb you are examining.

The average length of the thumb is about the same length as the little finger. Held close to the hand, its tip should reach at least the middle of the base phalange of the index finger. If it is longer than this, it can be called a long thumb; if shorter, a short thumb.

## Short Thumb

In general a short or underdeveloped thumb indicates a lack of character and difficulty in controlling or mastering the environment. The very small and underdeveloped thumb is a well-known feature of people with Down's syndrome.

## Long Thumb

A long and well-formed thumb indicates a strong character who is assertive and very much in control of his or her environment. But we must take a closer look at the components of the thumb to gain a more detailed interpretation.

## Ball of the Thumb

This is the source of the basic energies supplied to the thumb. Therefore the thumb itself depends on the power and support of this base. The ball of the thumb indicates very instinctive drives and life energies, which can tell us about the person's vitality, physical strength, and sexual drives.

## Phalanges of the Thumb

There are two phalanges in the thumb: the upper or first phalange, which is the end section of the thumb, and the lower or second phalange, which is the section between the end and the ball of the thumb.

When phalanges are described as long, broad, or thin, there is no specific measurement to define these characteristics. It is a case of personal judgment. The more hands you look at, the more easily you will be able to distinguish the characteristics of the phalanges.

### The Upper, First Phalange

This represents personal determination and action. By looking at the length, breadth, and form of this phalange, we can tell how capable the person is in expressing his or her own identity, implementing ideas, and making a personal impression in the outside world. It is important to be aware that this phalange is dependent on the energies supplied to it by the lower phalange and the ball of the thumb.

The length of this phalange will indicate the quality and degree to which the person is able to exercise his or her own will, influence other people, and alter his or her environment. When it is long, the quality and sophistication of the person's expression of action and identity in these areas are strong. These people will perform their actions with a good deal of skill and agility. The implementation and performance of ideas will be very important.

When this phalange is short, a certain amount of simplicity and even coarseness is indicated in the performance of action and the person's relationships with others. Such a person will need to use a great deal more effort to exert his or her will and determination in the world. There will tend to be a feeling of lack of identity in the world, and this is of great importance to the person.

The breadth of the first phalange indicates the amount of force or weight that is put into the action. When this phalange is very broad, it shows a great deal of strength in the performance of action and dominance in the expression of identity. Such people will impress others easily. If it is thin, the power of implementation is greatly lessened, and action will be achieved by more subtle methods, such as opportunism.

### The Lower, Second Phalange

This indicates reasoning abilities. By looking at the length and breadth of this phalange, we can tell how the subject will respond to reason and logic. This second phalange can be thought of as the conductor of power from the ball of the thumb through to the action of the first phalange. If this phalange is weak, the power of determination and ability to act expressed in the first phalange will be impaired. Therefore we must look to see the quality of energy this section is capable of providing.

The length of this phalange can reveal to us the

extent of reason and logic that is used in our actions. The shorter this phalange, the more crude is the energy passed on. Therefore, if it is short, the person will be unable to plan his or her actions by reason or logical thought, usually making quick and intuitive decisions.

If it is long and well formed, the person will tend to plan and think through ideas before putting them into action. The longer this phalange is, the more refined the energy, and so the person will respond well to reason and logic and will plan and deliberate before carrying out any actions.

It is important, however, not to forget the rule that applies throughout hand analysis. It is that any quality in excess can become a weakness. If the second phalange is very long, then the person will give excessive thought to his or her actions. This can greatly delay achievements. Conversely, if it is too short, the person will be overimpulsive and take his or her desires to excess.

The thickness of this phalange will show the quantity of energy provided by way of reason. This second phalange often has a slight "waist," but where there is significant waisting, it indicates a restriction of the energy flow. Reason and argument can often become an obstacle to this type of person, who can easily be influenced by logical argument or too readily questions the consequences of his or her own actions and therefore may compromise his or her original plans. This person will approach life with subtlety and diplomacy.

When this phalange is broad, the energy flows strongly and directly, and it is unlikely that these people can be deterred by others from their own plans or objectives. They are unlikely to compromise themselves and will be more direct in their approach to life.

## Length and Relationship Between the Phalanges

The two phalanges should ideally be of equal length to give a good balance of both action and thought. When one is clearly dominant over the other, the obvious interpretation can be made.

### Longer First Phalange

For example, if the first phalange is longer than the second, such people are likely to be people of action but lacking the backup of logic and reason to guide their actions. It is likely that they will do something just because that's what they want to do. Diplomacy and compromise will be unlikely to sway them in their path. If the first phalange is significantly longer and dominant, then they will want to dominate and enforce their ideas, and no amount of persuasion and reason will make them change their minds.

### Longer Second Phalange

If the second phalange is longer than the first, then such people are likely to give thought and planning before taking action. Logic and reason will influence how they carry out their actions. They will be more a thinker and a conceptual person than an action person. If the second phalange is significantly longer and dominant, then they may only conceptualize and action may play only a very small part in their lives.

## Flexibility of the Thumb Phalanges

The next quality to look for in the thumb is the amount of flexibility between the first and second phalanges. This is the amount the top of the thumb will bend back toward the wrist. The flexible thumb indicates people who are adaptable to new environments and new ideas; they tend to have easygoing natures and are able to change their plans or courses of action quickly and frequently if a better or preferred way is found. Too much flexibility will mean the subjects may chop and change frequently in their plans and action. Too often they look for the easiest ways out and want to please others around them.

## Little Flexibility of the Thumb Phalanges

The thumb that has little or no flexibility belongs to people who are not very adaptable and are cautious of new ideas and new environments. Their nature tends to be quite straight-backed and not so easygoing. They will tend to follow rules more rigidly and, once set on a course, are less likely to

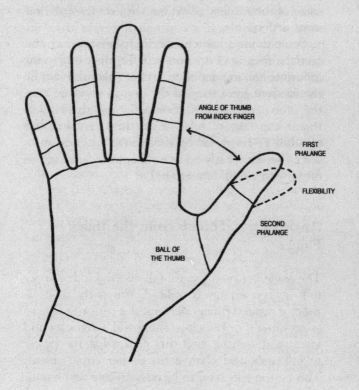

ANGLE OF THUMB
FROM INDEX FINGER

FIRST
PHALANGE

FLEXIBILITY

SECOND
PHALANGE

BALL OF
THE THUMB

*Angle of Thumb and Flexibility of Thumb Phalanges*

alter. Often they may take the long way around because of their inflexibility, but they are nevertheless more dependable.

Some thumbs have no flexibility whatsoever and give the feeling of an iron rod. This person is very inflexible and unadaptable, and at times this can be the cause of great stress if the person involved is in the wrong environment. Someone with this kind of thumb can take to rules or doctrine very well but also can be restricted by those rules and find himself or herself clearly on one side of the fence or the other with no middle ground.

## Angle of the Thumb from the Index Finger

The angle between the thumb and the index finger tells us how energy is utilized. When the angle is wide, at around ninety degrees, the person is able to assert himself or herself in the world. Character and identity are strong, and this person has the power to influence and change his or her environment. This person will tend to be adventurous and impulsive.

If the angle is more than ninety degrees, the person may be careless and overimpulsive, lacking sensible caution and control in exercising his or her energies.

When the angle is acute and the thumb can only be moved a little way from the index finger, the person will be naturally cautious. This reveals a surrendering of power and an inability to change or influence his or her environment. These people can easily be influenced by others and by their environment and can often be found living within strong religious or moral doctrines or in effect surrendering their own self-determination. The smaller the angle, the more these qualities will manifest within the person.

## The Thumb's Point of Emergence

A thumb coming from the lowest section of the hand reveals a practical, dependable expression of mind. If it emerges from the highest level, it reveals a childish and often more physically oriented frame of mind. The central position is most common and reveals a balance of impression (see illustration, page 76).

## An Intuitive Look at the Thumb

Two images may help describe the quality and power of the human thumb and its place in our psyche. The first is that people's thumbs are like little sprouts, something that's growing, a plant. The second is that the thumb is stuck in the soil like a seed. It puts out roots, and from it the person grows or sprouts. The roots of the growing thumb are reaching out into the world, into society. So looking at a person's thumb gives us some idea of what level of growth that person has reached, what point he or she has reached socially, what his or her status is. The thumb in essence is a symbol of hu-

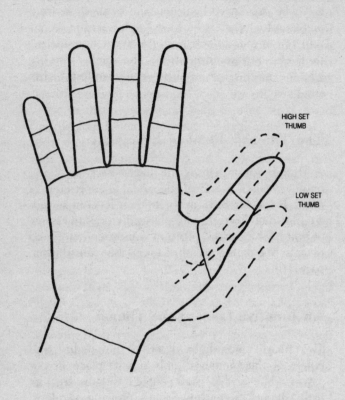

HIGH SET
THUMB

LOW SET
THUMB

*The Thumb's Point of Emergence*

man status. It depicts our personalities, our uniqueness, and what mark we leave on the world in living our lives. Its strength shows what makes us stand out. Its weakness depicts the characteristics that lead to our merging into the crowd. So it indicates our standing in connection with other human beings, where we place ourselves or where others place us because of their relationship with us.

In looking at the thumb, we should look to see what is happening at the roots of the thumb, the part that connects to the palm and almost to the wrist. If you think of the thumb as a plant, as something that has grown, this area is of great importance. If that area shows diminished development, if that area is hurt, then the very roots of the personality, the very roots of how this particular person is in the world, or how he or she is realizing themselves in the world, are weak. If such people haven't strong roots, they haven't got good foundations to their identities. They might very well achieve reasonably well, but it will be at quite a cost. They will have to work harder than anyone else. They haven't the resources that people with strong roots have.

With a really powerful fundamental base, with a healthy-looking ball of the thumb and palm in that area, then the source out of which the personality has grown, the richness of the soil, as it were, is very strong and resourceful. For such people, their unconscious sense of themselves, their competence, their feeling of connection with their bodies, their connection with how they relate through their bodies to the rest of the world is a good one. It is sound, but what builds on from there might be quite different and might be not as strong as a person with a weak base.

The structure of the thumb as it emerges from the hand shows how it channels what has gone before. Still using the image of the growing plant, we note that if the second phalange, the one between the tip and the hand, is really wide, like a healthy plant stem, then it is allowing a lot of energy to flow through. It's almost like a river without any dam on it. The water just flows, whereas if there is some definable shape in that area, then it's like a control; there is some measure of restraint. It filters the energy or flow.

The actual ball of the thumb—the top of it—is huge in its sensitivity. It has a lot of nerve endings. We tend to think of our contact with the world being through the tips of our fingers, but actually it is through the first finger and the tip of the thumb. It is the area we appraise things with. We assess them, we test them, we touch them, we feel them in some way, and we gauge our relationship with what we are touching. So the tip of the thumb is a receiving agent and is also associated with leaving our imprint or our mark on the world. Something of us grows through the thumb into the world.

Because it is the essence of who we are, our subtlety, our grossness, our strength and weakness all leave their imprint on the world through the thumb. If you think of how you grasp something— it might be a broomstick or a door handle—the fingers grasp it, unless it's a small object, but the thumb is on top of it. We then have a hold on the thing. We have left a mark on it, and it's our mark.

If that area is weakly developed, the person's energy doesn't flow out to grasp the world so powerfully. This is why we use the phrase "to get a grasp on" something to mean understanding or connecting with it. Someone "loses his grip" if he loses power in his activities. Whatever we take hold of in life, whatever we do leaves a mark. Everything leaves a mark; trees leave a mark on the environment as they take up nutrients in the soil and change them, then release them altered. Human beings do the same; they alter things. Because we each have a mind and emotions, we alter it in a variety of ways, and because of an individual's particular qualities, the mark he leaves on the world is recognizably his, like his handwriting and fingerprints.

If we translate these factors connected with the thumb into the less physical side of ourselves, we see that the thumb connects with our unique identity and how we impress ourselves upon the world.

# 5

## The Fingers

Fingers say a lot about the hand. Fingers work in two ways. Not only do we take in information from the world when we grasp things—we touch, we sense, we feel with our fingers—but also we express outwardly with our fingers. We create in the world, and the fingers are the expression of our creativity. We make and manipulate things with our fingers. So there is a two-way flow: what we have put out and what we take in. In this way the fingers are the communication between the outside world and all the qualities that are represented in the rest of the palm. The fingers are the link.

Think of fingers as channels of energy outward to the world and receivers from the world inward. When looking at a person's fingers, ask yourself what those fingers do. What are they receiving, what are they putting out?

When we look at the fingers, as with the thumb, we must look at their quality. When I look at fingers, I first try to look at the form and the overall character of them. As with the rest of the hand, assess your response to what the fingers look like, what sort of quality of feeling they arouse in you. For instance, some fingers may look as if they have not been cared for, or they are an odd shape. Sometimes fingers give the sense of being twisted, or perhaps give you the sense of strength, or that strength is missing. All these things say something about the fingers and the person. So generally, when looking at hands and in the analysis of hands, always remember the first thing is to look at their quality, look at what they tell you without any analytical views or rules and without applying the information that you have learned. Be conscious of what you feel about the area of the hand you are observing.

## The Length of the Fingers

After being aware of your response to a person's fingers, you next analyze their length. The length of fingers shows us the distance between the inner self and the person's expression to the outside world.

The length of the fingers is important in the Chinese method of categorizing hand shape. The length of the fingers helps determine what type or shape a hand is. Fingers can be either long or short, and in most cases by looking at the length of the fingers in relation to the size of the palm, we can quickly assess their size. In cases where there is doubt, a good guide to follow is if the length of the middle finger is over three quarters of the length of the palm, then the fingers are long. If the middle finger is less than three quarters of the length of the palm, then the fingers can be called short.

Measure the length of the middle finger from its tip to the line at the base. If you then start from the line at the base of the middle finger and see how far this measurement takes you down the palm, you can see whether the classification is long, short, or medium. Each of these classifications has attached to it certain character traits as follows:

## Short Fingers

These people tend to be motivated by their feelings. Physical and material activities and interests predominate in them. They are people of action; they have alert and quick minds, enjoy organizing but dislike work involving any great detail.

Short-fingered people are impatient; they work from emotions and are emotional people; they are organizing people; they are people who like to be part of groups. Usually they are down-to-earth and realistic about life. Because of the short fingers, there is less of a distance between their inner selves, their personas, and the outside world, so who they are is coming out to the world in a much stronger and sometimes even cruder manner. In general the short-fingered people work more from an emotional, intuitive, or instinctive perspective.

It's interesting that contrary to expectation, people with short fingers and usually small hands are not capable of doing very intricate work, yet people with long fingers and large hands are the people who can. It is something that at first seems to be the wrong way around. But long-fingered people can do detailed work because they consider and plan their actions a great deal more, and there is a lot more space between their thoughts and actions.

## Long Fingers

People with long fingers tend to be motivated by the conceptual, mental, and analytical activities. They are people who think and plan and are cautious when it comes to actions or decisions. They enjoy work requiring mental and analytical qualities or work that involves great detail and care. They are good communicators.

People with long fingers tend to be more thoughtful, tend to work at a slower pace, to be more idealistic, and to be the thinkers of the world. Long-fingered people are inclined to think about things before they act, and there is a greater space between who and what they are and their expression of that in the outside world.

What it comes down to is that there is much less space—the buffer between thought and action—in short-fingered people. Short-fingered people work in a very immediate world. Long-fingered people are working on the basis of planning and thinking ahead.

## Medium-size Fingers

You will generally be able to classify fingers as being long or short, and this will become easier with experience, but if you really can't tell which they are, then try to look at the other areas of the hand to help you classify it as one of the four hand types. If you are satisfied that you have identified the hand type, then call the fingers long or short depending on the hand type you have chosen.

Fingers that in all respects seem to be medium-size will carry a balance between the qualities of long and short fingers, a balance between emotion/intuition and thinking/planning. In a hand reading we are really looking to classify the areas of the hand as one thing or another if at all possible to prevent the reading from becoming vague and general. We are looking for characteristics, symptoms, and imbalances to be able to interpret the person correctly. So try to get into the habit of committing yourself to a classification, whichever area of the hand you are looking at, so you can understand the leanings or inclinations of those qualities represented. The classification may have to be chosen by the smallest of margins.

## Thick and Thin Fingers

Another thing to consider about fingers is whether they are thick or thin. Each finger should be looked at individually, but also you can look to see if generally the fingers are thick or thin. It helps to understand the analysis of the hand if we think of fingers as channels of energy, channels of expression.

## Thick Fingers

Thick-fingered people tend to be powerful in their expression. They are inclined to be quite conservative or conventional people.

I tend to think of thick fingers as being like the huge pillars that hold up a temple. These thick fingers are like pillars, and people with them tend to be pillars of society. They are the farmers, the soldiers, the politicians, people who uphold the most basic things in society. They have a lot of strength, a lot of stamina. They express themselves with a lot of energy, and they are very solid and realistic in what they are and do.

## Thin Fingers

Thin-fingered people are capable of expressing and receiving much less energy. If the fingers are very thin, we can see a character that possibly cannot stand up against the forces of the world, that does not have that much stamina and can be easily shaken or disturbed. Such a person may be a servant of the rules and customs of society or a person who, to survive, has to get around those rules. If he cannot do that, he may live outside the rules or find ways around them.

Thin-fingered people seldom have the strength to meet the experiences and demands of life in the same way as the thick-fingered person.

In general a person's fingers have similar thicknesses. But that is not always the case, and you may find one finger that is slightly thinner or thicker than the others. Therefore the fingers must be observed individually because there is a lot of information to be gained from each one.

## Finger Length

In order to judge whether fingers are long or short, one needs some idea of what is considered normal. If we number the fingers from the thumb, the index finger would be number one, the finger next to it number two, the ring finger number three, and the little finger number four. This makes it clear what finger is being discussed. The normal order of length is as follows:

- The longest finger is number two.
- The first finger is normally the next longest, its tip coming to the middle of the top phalange of the second finger.
- The third finger is next. Its normal length is to just below the middle of the top phalange of the second finger.
- The tip of the fourth finger reaches to the line at the base of the top phalange of the third finger.

So to judge length and to take the fourth finger as an example, if its tip reaches above the line at the base of the top phalange of the third finger, then it would be considered long. If its tip reached well above this line to the middle of the top phalange of the third finger, it would be very long. The reverse would also be true for shortness.

Looking at my own hands, if I hold my hands flat and palms up, I can immediately see that my third finger is longer than my first finger on my right hand; it reaches well above the middle of the second finger. On my left hand, however, the finger lengths are more normal, except that my first finger is well above the middle of the second finger and the third easily reaches the middle of the second finger. Such observation shows the unique character of each hand and indicates the particular areas of full development or lack of power in each person.

## The First Finger

The first finger or index finger is known as the finger of Jupiter. The Chinese symbolism for this finger is Water. This finger represents the amount of personal self-esteem a person has, the amount of drive and confidence he has in projecting himself forward into the outside world. This is the finger we point with; it is a directive finger; it can even be rude to point with this finger because it is representative of us and our ego. I know that the thumb represents our ego, but this finger concerns more of who we are in the outside world, projecting ourselves and our confidence in ourselves.

## Long First Finger

If this finger is long, and at times it can be almost as long as the second finger, such people have a great deal of confidence. They rarely like being told what to do. They would rather lead others and can have a certain amount of arrogance. They can be domineering and dogmatic. People with long and even strong and straight index fingers show an ability to go forward and be directive in the things they want to do. They stand forward as a person and stand up to others. This length shows directiveness in life and the ability to stand their ground and have a good feeling about themselves.

## Short First Finger

When this finger is short, it indicates a person lacking in confidence. It can be considered short when it only just reaches the base of the top phalange of the second finger or slightly above. People with short first fingers may act proud because of their lack of self-esteem or confidence. They may be people who are quite fussy and are easily upset by something that might make them look small or inferior in any way. People with short index fingers, and it is quite noticeable in the hand when this finger is short, are lacking in the power to stand their ground. They seldom feel good about themselves and often fail to project themselves forward into society.

There is a possibility that people with short index fingers may try to get around the rules of society because their self-esteem is low. They may have fewer scruples in going about getting what they want or have lower standards to uphold personally. They may also exaggerate things or put on a show because they find difficulty in living up to what they feel is acceptable. They can easily become snobs.

This finger, the finger of Jupiter, when it is strong certainly gives the person independence and the ability to stand apart from others in being himself and in taking his own views on things and saying with confidence, "This is who I am; this is what I am doing."

Obviously if this finger is leaning against the second finger, then it would rely on or be supported by the qualities of the second finger, and its strength is reduced. If it is growing toward or bending toward the second finger, for example, the person's self-esteem would be expressed through the qualities of the second finger; this reduces the independence of the first finger.

## The Second Finger

The second finger is known as the finger of Saturn in the Western astrological system, and in the Chinese elemental system it is the Earth finger. It is a finger of balance, being in the middle of the hand, and represents balance within the person. This finger tells us of the inner world of the character as it is expressed outwardly.

In 99 percent of people this finger is the longest on the hand. It tells us of the conventional side of the character, the ability the person has to respond to law, to rules. It indicates family, duty, and the things we carry as responsibility in our lives. It connects with things that have deep and fundamental origins within us and that provide the balance and certainty in our lives that we must take care of and responsibility for.

It is the finger that represents logic and reasoning and that goes together with its position of balance within the hand. It is a supportive finger. Even its physical positioning on the hand suggests this, for it is not a digit that alone sees any action but one that is always involved right in the middle of all the fingers' activity. This finger shows the basis of a person, his makeup and the responsibility he can take on, the importance of his family and those things that are very much supportive within his life.

## Long Second Finger

People with long second fingers may be good at running their own businesses, taking on responsibility, and having a good solid basis of character. They will form good links with their community and be regarded as dependable and socially mature.

If this finger is large and well formed, the roots of the person are very good. The ability to take on responsibility, to respect the laws and the customs of society is good. It also points to the balance of the character, so it shows a sufficient degree of balance, being like the anchor finger within the palm.

## Short Second Finger

The finger is short if it fails to rise much above the two fingers next to it. In this case it indicates a person who is unwilling to take on the sorts of responsibilities people usually meet as they mature. He would find it difficult to accept the responsibility of children or a marriage partner. In some ways such people may be immature or dependent in that their stance and drives might be very self-centered rather than their lives' being connected with others in a more balanced way.

## The Third Finger

The third or ring finger is known as the finger of Apollo or the Sun in the astrological system, and in the Chinese elemental system it is the Fire finger.

This finger connects with our creativity. It is about what we externalize in our lives and about our energy and our drive to create. This is the expression of the person more in raw energy terms. When we look at a hand and see the tendencies within that character—whether they are physical or artistic in some way or intellectual—this finger represents the expression of those tendencies, the expression of creativity in that individual.

Generally this finger is the third-longest finger on the hand. Normally the second finger is the longest, the index or first finger the second-longest, and the ring or third finger the third-longest. The little or fourth finger is always the shortest, hence its name. Variations to that combination obviously have meanings that can be interpreted accordingly.

This finger is less deliberate and conscious than the thumb and the first two fingers, so in that sense it has to do with many of the interactions that go on between us and other people that are less deliberate, that are semiconscious in a way. Many people don't recognize those factors in their lives—the emotional or social factors that although barely conscious are extremely powerful.

So this finger is partly unconscious. It represents the unconscious because in its physical form it is less determined than the thumb and first two fingers. It is more spontaneous. But it is still to do with contact because it is reaching out, still making contact with the world out there, but it is less deliberate contact than the other parts of the hand that we hold with, so we can understand its function from that point of view.

## Long Third Finger

Sometimes this finger is as long as the index finger and sometimes longer, making it the second-longest finger on the hand. If this finger is long and well developed, it shows a powerful drive in the tendencies that the person has or possesses in his hand. So with a person who is quite physical it will show someone with an excessive amount of physical energy and maybe a very strong sex drive. He or she may not need very much sleep and is likely to be very active.

I see this finger as indicating whether or not

someone has a lot of emotion in his hand; with a long third finger we can say the emotions are expressed strongly and creatively. In an intellectual hand then a long third finger shows a strong intellectual creativity. So the finger shows the degree of our creativity, and to some extent it shows our ability for success as far as our creativity is involved in that success.

It is notable that people with long and well-developed third fingers tend to have a lot of energy, are outgoing, expressive, and talkative in their interests, and physically have strong drives. In many textbooks on hand analysis, a long third finger can mean a very strong sexual drive. My own experience with people suggests that this is not necessarily always true, but it can be the result if that is the area the subject lives through or for.

People with long third fingers have an ability to communicate themselves, an ability to put across their ideas and views, and also an ability to communicate with others within personal and emotional relationships.

### Short Third Finger

If short, this finger shows a lack of ability to express oneself creatively. Such people may be lacking in physical energy and "get up and go" and need a lot of sleep. They may not express themselves emotionally to any great degree. These people will tend to lack creativity in the more personal part of themselves, and their way of expressing themselves will be seen in a more crude and basic way.

## The Fourth Finger

The fourth or little finger is known as the finger of Mercury and in Chinese symbolism is the Air finger. It represents how we communicate ourselves to the outside world, our ability to be fluent in communication. In Victorian times, when one drank tea, the fourth finger was stuck out to show refinement, and this says something about the fourth finger, about etiquette, conduct, and social interaction.

At times this finger can be seen to jut out and is quite independent and away from the other fingers. This shows a strong and independent side to the person in expressing and communicating himself. These people may have strong and original views on things, or something they particularly need to communicate is quite strong within them. This expression is normally unconventional, and unconventional relationships are also often found in people with this jutting-out fourth finger, whereas if the finger is held very close to the third finger, then communication is not as independent and is more conventional.

### Large or Long Fourth Finger

If this finger is long or well formed, the subject shows a good ability to communicate with others. These people tend to be quite articulate. They may be good speakers or writers or work well in the media or any form of communication that is shared socially. A large or long fourth finger also indicates people who have a maturity within relationships and can interact well with others socially. They have a good ability to communicate and share their own ideas with society.

### Small Fourth Finger

People with a short fourth finger—and it is noticeably short if its tip reaches only the middle of the second phalange of the third finger—may have difficulty in communicating. Sometimes they can be quite childlike and immature in relating to others because they cannot easily make themselves understood. So at times they may have childish tantrums or frustration because—and maybe they have not realized it—people have not understood what they are trying to communicate.

## An Intuitive Look at the Fingers

In the hands you have the whole history of human life and evolution. They still carry on the basic functions of putting food to our mouths, scratching our behinds, hitting fellow creatures, and grabbing hold of their hair and banging their heads on the ground. People are still doing that. They are still picking up a stick or stone and whacking somebody with it. But we have carried it on from there. If we were to create an image of all the things that the hands do, then we would have an idea what the fingers connect with. They are the complete range of these possibilities, everything from grabbing a piece of food to hanging from a branch to playing a piano to carrying out operations using microsurgery or etching some electronic equipment—all that extension of being, that extension of life. They are the paintbrush of the soul, the tools of life.

There is something that has to be said about the fingers. If it is not said, there is something missing in their description. The fingers had a life long before human beings existed. They lived, they were part of life on this world, and they had to do with the gaining of greater control over food and movement. So they are not peculiar to human beings, but their past is something we have taken up and carried forward, so that we developed opposability in the thumb. But the fingers were always there, delicately shaped and formed. They were already waiting for us to take them and glorify them.

In an odd way they are the ground, the potential out of which the opposable thumb emerged. They called to the thumb to come forth, and this is important in the nature of human beings and in the structure of the single fingers. The ability to integrate yet separate arose. Thus they can work together or they can work separately, and that is something that hadn't happened previously to this extent in the animal kingdom. It was almost like having legs on the end of your legs. A spider might move one leg at a time, we might move one limb at a time, but then to have limbs on the end of your limbs added a tremendous new dimension of ability to relate to the physical world in quite a different way. The dog or the cat could pick up its babies and carry them and move them around, but the ape could pull its fleas out. It could hold a stick and manipulate it in quite a different way, and this is what the fingers could build; this is the platform from which we are able to touch the world, move it, direct it in a different way. This past is still evident in our hands. The fingers are the lengths they are because of the way our forebears used them. They are the connection that we have with them.

This has a particular meaning for human beings. It is one of the areas of human life that has not developed very far from the apes. The pelvis has changed, the head has changed, the arms and legs have changed, the spine has changed, the genitals have changed, the breasts have changed, even the thumb has changed, but the fingers aren't so different. When we are looking at the fingers, we are looking at our past. We are looking at how human beings have fundamentally related to the world for millions of years. The hands and the fingers link us with our forebears much more thoroughly than most other aspects of our lives because of the tasks that we still do with them.

So when I define the fingers, in general I would say that from them life developed a quality that wasn't expressed on the earth beforehand. There is a quality in the fingers relating to the physical world, with changing things, with being able to manipulate, being able to create, to take hold of the world and reshape it in an enormous variety of ways, much more so than other creatures. Along this line of development came the thumb. The fingers were like musical instruments, and suddenly, when the thumb came, they began to play. They were playing before in an unaccomplished way, but

when the thumb emerged in its present form, di-
mensions of music emerged that had been un-
thought of previously.

Consciousness was there, but the fingers enabled
it to extend, to refine itself, to open aspects of itself
that were not there before. Through the fingers we
actually leave a record of ourselves in the world, on
the world, in stone, in wood, in print, in the shape
of things.

If people have thin fingers, they are making a
statement through their bodies. They are saying,
"I'm barely capable of living. Things in life are
threatening to me, and therefore I will experience
life through my thoughts and plans." It may be that
these people have some difficulty in their actual
bodies. They may have been born with some physical difficulties or their bodies are not very strongly
developed. This may have been why they learned
to control life remotely or deal with it two paces
back or through somebody else. This thinness is not
to be confused with long fingers or short fingers.

If people have thick, powerful fingers, it means
they have a lot of physical presence; they express
more powerfully through their physical selves,
through enjoying physical contact, through relish-
ing food, through being involved sexually. They are
ready for more direct contact and rough-and-tum-
ble with other people. That is not to say they all
are strong people. The thick finger doesn't indicate
that they all are well balanced and everyone else is
not well balanced; that is different. Overall it involves the amount of body they expose to life, how
much of themselves they dare to develop and in-
volve in a direct way with the physical world. It

can be seen in how much contact with life, how much of their flesh is going to contact the world, how much of themselves they have allowed to flower.

A different personality type is indicated by short fingers. There are aspects of the short-fingered person that are not being allowed to develop. There is a lot of such a person that has not flowered, that is not allowed. These people may have accepted childhood restraints regarding their behavior, and so a great deal of what may have emerged of their personalities remains undeveloped. It is still there inside them. They have that potential, but something happened to them that stops them from really developing. Or they have an attitude that makes them live what others want of them. They are full human beings in a certain sense, but as far as extending themselves, developing that extra something in life, that extra expressiveness, creativity, conversation, that extra sparkle that really make them quite a distinct person, that isn't allowed. They have taken a stance of being ultraconservative. They have made a decision perhaps unconsciously to play things safe. In "doing the right thing," they have withheld themselves, whereas with the long-fingered person it is the inquisitiveness, the expressiveness, the extraordinary exploration of fate that characterize them.

Any or all of these can be transcended. Each human being has a possibility of transcending its fate as it is expressed in its body. Each person can transcend what he has become, what he has built, what has been created at this level. People can go beyond that. This would actually produce some changes in the hand, although it wouldn't necessarily mean that the short fingers would become very lengthy. But it would produce marks in the hand, a flowing of lines toward the fingers, connectivity between the lines of the hands, and the integration of the different aspects of the hands through the lines.

# 6

## Phalanges, Nails, Skin, and Rings

### The Phalanges

Making up all of the fingers are three phalanges: base, middle, and top.

#### The Base Phalange

This is the phalange nearest the palm. It shows us the base and roots of the quality of the finger. If the bottom phalange has a waist and is thin, then we can see that the basis and expression of the finger's quality are impaired and the energy flow to the rest of the finger is deficient. This can give us an indication of the real underlying strength of the quality of a particular finger.

If the base phalange is large or fat, then we can see that finger has a strong base and quite a lot of energy at its root level, but we must look to see if

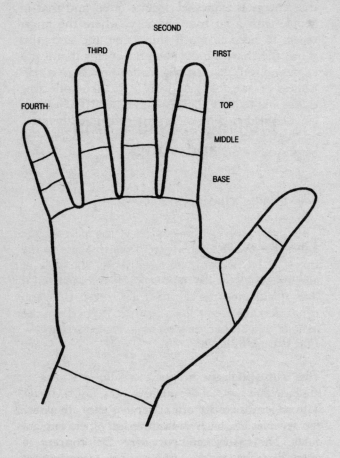

*Fingers and Phalanges*

that energy is expressed. I quite often find that in people with a fat base phalange, where the finger tapers to become much thinner at the end, this shows they have a lot of potential energy that is not expressed well. It therefore tends to result in a self-ishness or greed or causes them to like collecting things and to have things around them. Their energies are held close to them rather than be liberated, and this often shows in their life as a tendency to be possessive and materialistic.

## The Middle Phalange

This deals with action, and it is the part of the finger that transmits the power from the base to the tip. If it has a waist, it is restricting the flow of action and expression and incoming information. If it is thick, then the flow is good, the action and expression are strong, and the ability to perform the actions that the finger represents is also strong.

## The Top Phalange

The fingertips are important because they are where we receive information and actually perform actions. The touch, the conceiving, the concept of everything that we do start here. The receptivity of the fingertips is also important. The longer and larger they are, the more receptive that person is. If the pads of the fingertips have what look like drop-lets on them, showing the pad to be built up, rising to a point, this shows accentuated sensitivity, a good tactile sense, and great receptivity. If the pads are flat and coarse, the receptiveness is reduced. If the fingertips are quite thin—thinner than the rest of the finger—then receptivity and expression are low.

One thing that is noticeable with fingertips is that sometimes they have a spatulate shape, which means the end of the fingers actually widen, and this shows quite a strong and fiery expression of energy.

## An Intuitive Look at Phalanges

The fingers are the means of accomplishing the finer points of the desire to manipulate the world. We can grasp tools; we can tie and untie knots; we can perform these actions with such precision and diversity of motives and emotions that it is easy to see the fingers are our physical means of self-expression.

The phalanges have a particular relationship with this general view of the fingers. The phalanges are rather like stages in this world of self-expression. The base phalange is the one nearest the palm. We can think of this as being like the foundations of a house. This phalange connects with the framework, the broad plans of our actions.

Out of this develops the middle phalange, which has to do with materialization, giving something form, bringing it into shape, and making it known so that it can be seen and experienced through the senses.

The end or top phalanges of the fingers are concerned with shaping and refining what first of all has its foundation in the base phalange and formation in the middle phalange. So those are the three aspects of the phalanges: foundation, formation, and refinement.

Coming back to the base phalanges, I want to attempt a clear definition of how this idea of foundation comes about because it is quite a philosophical point. It can be made plain, however, by the trick already used to illustrate other points—the imagined removal of parts of the hand. If you cut off the top two joints of the fingers, this gives you an idea of what these phalanges represent. You would be able to do very much less with your hands. You might be able to shape something, you might be able to grasp something, you might be able to move it, but it would be much more difficult to do or sense the finest things that are done with the tips of the fingers; that would be lost. It is in the tips of the fingers that the delicate aspects of our self-expression are manifested. Consider touching someone with the stubs of your fingers. Even if they were rounded like the tips of your fingers, there would be a lack of delicacy, a lack of response, a lack of springiness compared to the sort of refined contact with the world the fingertips give, and this is the basis of the definition of foundation, formation, and refinement.

As for the middle joints, their definition also has a basis in the physical world in that they have a flexibility. They work as a go-between, a channeling, a conduit between the foundation and the refinement. The middle phalanges give the tips of the fingers the mobility and ability to do their work and their craft. They help shape the actions of the fingertips.

In each person's hand these phalanges have a variety of shapes and sizes. The phalanges relate to how people experience themselves, how they actualize themselves. They indicate how people are built up, how they themselves have come into being, and how they will express themselves externally. This in turn denotes how they will make things come into being.

Therefore the phalanges have a direct relationship to how things come into existence or how we ourselves make things happen. If there is a very long phalange close to the hand, this means the person has a lot of primal energy, a lot of creative power. But unless the other phalanges are of the same length, this is a suppressed energy, a frustrated power in that person. The force isn't transferred out of the fingers. It stays in, almost like physical vitality that can't find a means of expression. It might even become an irritation, an irritant, an angry energy, an energy that lashes out because it cannot delicately create. So that shaped phalange, a long-base phalange, can represent that sort of character, one whose energy is pent up and expresses without grace, without refinement.

If the base phalanges are very short and the other phalanges longer, then it is quite the reverse. It is almost as if the people did not have a lot of creativity but what they did with what they have is full of craft, very skilled. They would be the sort of person who takes up the ideas of others and makes them beautiful or skillfully expresses them. But they themselves lack the sort of dynamism that the shaping or foundry power of the long-base phalanges have. People who have short base phalanges and long fingertips in an odd way are receptive to the world. They lack their own inner direction very often, their own internal power, but they do seem to gain power from the world. It is almost as if they waited for the world to shape them, as if they waited for the direction in their life to come from external factors. Therefore they are very connected to events in the world. They are people who have a great deal of knowledge about the world. It means so much to them; it is almost as if it were the center of their lives. They look upon it as if it were their own memory, as if it contained in it the secrets of their own lives, and in a way it does.

So if the base and top phalanges are long and the middle phalanges are short, there is a mixture, a strange mixture. These people are often malcontents of this world. They have both a great deal of internal power and a contact with the world, but their ability to form this, to make anything of it is lacking. Often they become not necessarily criminals but certainly people who feel dispossessed. They feel sometimes as if life had done them down, as if it had taken away something from them.

This in fact has an advantage if they could use it. They have the possibility of taking their internal power and allowing others to express it. If they could do this, they would find a way of bridging this gap, of overcoming the weakness in their area of formation. However, because of their long top phalanges, they feel they have this ability themselves and that they ought to do it; they ought to be the ones with their fingers on the world, making it, shaping it. Unfortunately they don't have such an ability, and because they lack that connection, it would be better for them if they could find humility enough to allow others to act for them.

In looking at the phalanges, I sense also that there is something about their shape and not just their length that is very important. Some people have fingers that are parallel; they don't dip in and out. With other people it is quite the reverse. It looks as if their knuckles swelled out and they were weak in between, and this is an important factor in understanding the creative energy in people. It is another indication of how a person's energy is expressed.

The people whose fingers are parallel or tubular are very capable in their self-expression. Their ability to express themselves in the world is very powerful. It has a lot of qualities in it that make them recognized by others and accepted. Often they become the privileged in the world. It obviously depends on other qualities too, but there is a grace about them as if life had blessed them. This is how it may seem; they have things that other people lack.

People with fingers that do not have this rodlike shape but have indentations almost, expressive of the narrows in a river where energy builds up and then swirls out again, are no less creative or capable. It means their inner lives have more diversity, more tension, more currents. If they master diversity, they can be even greater figures in the world than those with tubular fingers. But often their inner diversity can become an adversity in their lives.

It is something they may not be able to manage,
and a lot of their energy or resources is taken up in
attempting to deal with this current, its changes
and shifts in their inner lives. Externally this is less
marked, less known, less self-expressed.

## The Fingernails

The nails depict our public faces, our professional
or social lives. They reveal the side of our nature
shown to the outer world.

When you study fingernails, look at them as if
you were examining the public face, the social and
professional side of the person. Look at the quality
of this aspect of the personality by seeing how the
nails are kept. The condition of the nails shows
what sort of person comes across in public.

### Large Nails

The larger the nail, or the larger the area of good-
quality nail, the better or more capable a public
face the person has. This means these people have
an ability to face people and to stand up in public
with confidence and present a good image of themselves.

### Small Nails

Nails that do not have a large area on top of the
finger tend to belong to shy people who have more

difficulty in communicating publicly. They do not have a great deal of power in creating a good public image.

### Bitten Nails

People who bite their nails show there is a weakness in their confidence when facing other people. It shows a person who suffers a more than average degree of anxiety and stress in meeting the demands of public life.

### Painted Nails

Nails that are painted (more commonly in women) show the desire to have a particular public face or to disguise the personality in some manner.

### Cared-for Nails

I feel nails that are well kept, have a good quality, and are clean and look reasonably well manicured show people who are fairly fastidious about how they are seen in public. They are likely to be more aware than most people of the importance of personal appearance and take care how they portray themselves.

## Uncared-for Nails

Nails that have dirt underneath them or do not seem to have a good and cared-for quality about them show somebody who is less aware of his public face or is less concerned about how he comes across.

## Flecks on the Nails

Nails normally take about six months to grow fully from the bottom of the nail to the tip. They grow faster in long-fingered people than they do in short-fingered people, and they grow faster on the long fingers than they do on the shorter fingers of the hand. But on average their growth takes about six months.

White flecks on the nails are a sign, in my experience, of some sort of nervous shock to the system or upheaval in the person's life or of nutritional deficiency. You can judge when this happened by considering the length of time the nails take to grow. If the fleck was right in the middle of the nail, for instance, then whatever caused the fleck would have occurred about three months before.

You can gather clues to the area of the person's life in which this disturbance occurred by looking at which finger the white flecks appear on. For instance, if the flecks are on the third finger, the stress would more likely be in connection with the person's creativity.

People with a lot of frequently occurring white flecks in their nails tend to live with a lot of stress or always have nutritionally deficient diets. These people tend to show signs of their stress publicly and may have other conditions connected with stress, such as psoriasis. I find this a very accurate way of identifying points of stress or change in a person's life.

I remember looking at one particular woman's hands and seeing a clear, well-marked white fleck on the nail of the second finger. It looked as if it had occurred about two months earlier. Because it was marked on the second finger, which represents family and responsibility, I suggested to her that she had had an upset or shock two months before and probably something to do with her family. She told me that her father had died exactly two months back; we identified this as causing the white fleck on the nail.

## Fingernail Moons

Moons on the fingernails represent the health of the heart. If these are on the large side, they are traditionally said to be a sign of a tendency to high blood pressure and a faster- or stronger-beating heart. Small moons, or moons not showing at all, suggest low blood pressure and a slower-beating heart or possibly a weak heart. In the book *Chinese Hand Analysis* by Shifu Terence Dukes (Aquarian, 1988) it says, "If blood pressure is high the moon at the base of the nail will be larger than average. Small or non-existent moons indicate a lowered blood pressure caused usually by a lack of exercise.

Deficient nutritional intake can also affect the moons."

## An Intuitive Look at Fingernails

In each of us there is a strength, a power. If you think of this power as being like a battery, some people have more power, more battery life, more stored energy than other people. Fingernails express something of this energy in a person. A person whose battery is flat shows it in his nails. In people with lower levels of vitality, the nails will break or split more often.

There is a slightly different process going on with a woman's fingernails. Menstruation causes certain marks in the nails, reflecting her vitality in a different way from that of a man. In her nails this shows not as ridges but as irregularities at certain times. You can get an idea of this by thinking about the lines you see when a tree is cut down. The irregular spacing of the lines shows the changing growth rates of the tree. Likewise, when a woman's energy is low, she is stressed for that time, and this influences the growth rate of her nails. You would have to look quite closely to see. The actual growth lines are irregular at some points, and this would mean her vitality changes, shifts, or drops as she goes through a cycle of peaks and troughs. The shape of her nails is less important than those markings. The shape has more to do with the character of the person than her energy. The shape and the markings indicate different standards with regard to the nails.

If you look at a lot of hands, you will see that some nails have a long, thin appearance, and some have more of a squarer, flatter appearance. Thin nails are often more curved across their surfaces than are flatter, squarer nails. Within each of us there is a set of genes—guidelines for shaping certain parts of our body—so flat or curved nails arise from this genetic coding. The shape and curve of the nails are an indication of a person's characteristics, strengths. The broader, flatter nails indicate people with less inclination to feel hurt by the world, less inclination to be sensitive to other people or how other people deal with them.

The opposite is true of the long, thin fingernails. With these more sensitive people it is almost as if the outside world impinged on them physically and hurt them or pleased them more. With these people it is as if they were connected more to the outside world. That isn't so, but that is how it appears, as if external factors were inextricably linked with their internal feelings and thoughts, whereas people with broad, flat nails seem to have less of a connection with the outside world, so they are more independent of it in their inner lives.

The subject of fingernails has been given a lot of attention. There has been quite a lot written in medical studies, health care research, and patients' records in connection with fingernails. The central points arising from this research are that if a person has certain internal problems, perhaps the liver or kidneys, this shows in the fingernails. There is some sort of change and discoloration from the normal.

These diseases can often be related to different fingernails, and a ruddy sort of glow or color in the fingernails is altered (see Chapter 16). So if there is a radical alteration of color in the fingernails, there may be problems with the internal organs, particularly the organs concerned with digestion, in which case it would be wise to consult a doctor.

Another area that is important in considering fingernails has to do with the length of a person's life. This is because the fingernails indicate the state of the physical battery energy—that is, how many reserves a person has. If a person has enormous reserves of energy and vitality, in virtually every case the person has an enormous power in the fingernails. They look different; they look as if they were strong and not given to breaking easily, almost as if they could be claws. In the person who has less vitality, the fingernails sometimes look almost paperlike. They don't have that thickness and power that a person with great vitality has.

The length of the nails can also be indicative of the person's inner health and efficiency in dealing with stress. Signs of strength in the nails are often obvious because they survive breakage a lot more easily, so can grow quite long. If people chew their nails or keep them short, it may be difficult to tell. But often if they chew their nails, their energies are really being overspent by internal emotional stress, so that in itself is a sign of reduced power in their health.

## Skin Quality

The skin quality of the hands gives us an indication
of the sensitivity of the person. Skin is usually either rough or smooth or fine. Skin is very much in
public view. Skin acts as a barrier, and depending
on its quality, it allows more or less of the outside
or public world to penetrate us.

### Smooth, Fine Skin

Smooth and fine skin shows a greater sensitivity
within people and a refinement in the way they live
their lives. So even in people who may be rather
nasty, their negative qualities would be expressed in
a refined or sensitive manner. Soft-skinned people
tend to be more sensitive, more emotional and also
to dislike physical labor.

### Rough, Coarse Skin

People with quite rough skin tend to be more
coarse in the way they express themselves. The person with rough or hard skin is a lot less sensitive or
emotional and more likely to do physical labor or
enjoy physical labor. The expression "thick-
skinned" gives us an indication of the meaning of
the skin's coarseness or softness.

### Dry Skin

The skin can also be dry or quite damp. I usually find that dry skin tends to indicate less surface emotion and nervousness. People with dry skin can be quite clinical and technical at times, and they are good at communicating without showing any emotion and good at taking in information.

### Damp Skin

Damp-skinned people are more ready to show emotions and may be quite nervous. Their emotions or nervousness show through quite easily in their communication with other people and conduct.

### Elastic or Springy Skin

There is also a middle type of skin, which is an elastic or springy skin. This is often found in professional people, businesspeople, doctors, or lawyers. People with this type of skin have the ability to put their ideas into practice.

## Hand Temperature

When you read hands, another thing to be aware of is their warmth. Some people's hands are very cold, whereas other hands are quite warm or even hot.

## Warm Hands

People who have very warm hands often show an ability to be openly warm in relationships. They easily connect with other people and show their emotions in their behavior and speech. Warm hands usually show a very good circulation and a good or fast metabolism.

## Cold Hands

People with cold hands tend to be more shy and inhibited. They have difficulty in showing that warmth easily and openly in public. Cold hands are also a suggestion of poor circulation, and I have often found that people who smoke or have just had a cigarette have cold hands.

## Rings

Rings on fingers are quite important. The basic meaning of a ring on a finger is that it shows something is lacking in the properties of the finger on which the ring is worn. Of course rings, such as the wedding ring, that most people wear because of custom need not be interpreted. Rings worn on other fingers do have a meaning, however, and can be interpreted.

### Ring on the First or Index Finger

A ring on this finger suggests a lacking in self-esteem and difficulty in taking a direction. It is worn by people who are very concerned about other people's views of them. They often look like quite proud people, perhaps as a way of making up for their sense of inadequacy.

### Ring on the Second Finger

A ring on this finger shows a weakness or lack of connection with family relationships. This aspect of life is very important and may suggest deficiency of family support. This will influence the person's fundamental feelings of security, and so he may feel uncomfortable with responsibility and find family and social support very important to him. This is not a common finger to wear a ring on.

### Ring on the Third or Ring Finger

A ring on the third finger is not necessary to interpret unless there are numerous rings worn. In that case I would say that there is lack in the person's emotional life and a lack in creative energies. The lack in emotional life might be something like a feeling of not being loved despite obvious affection given by those close to the person.

### Ring on the Fourth or Little Finger

A ring on the little finger is generally an indication of someone who wants to seem independent sexually or within relationships. It denotes an insecurity in relationships or a lack of sexual confidence. A ring on this finger is often worn by men and increasingly by women. I also see this ring as suggesting these people can sometimes be promiscuous. They can be noncommittal or can act quite independently in their relationships. I see this ring as expressing a need to make up for an insecurity or a lack they may feel about themselves.

Homosexuals quite often wear rings on their little fingers to signify their orientation.

### Ring on the Thumb

Rings on thumbs are very rarely worn but can show something lacking in a person's identity. I tend to find people who wear rings on their thumbs need to identify themselves with a group or another person because they are so uncertain of themselves. They possibly are lacking in willpower or impulsive drive also.

It is a strange thing that people do tend to wear rings on particular fingers expressive of their particular character traits. They may wear a ring on one finger, and it feels very uncomfortable; I have quite often seen people change a ring from one finger to another because of this feeling of discomfort. The ring might even have fitted the original finger better, but the people will change it to another that feels a lot more comfortable. I believe this is because they need to enhance the power of that finger because of their personal lack in that area.

# 7

## The Lines

The lines on the hand show us the direction and quality of expression of the basic energies of our being. These lines on the palm should be thought of as passages or routes for the flow of energies across the hand from one quadrant to the next. The major lines on the hand represent the most basic energies, drives, or functions in ourselves, and they are always present in some form. For example, the lifeline represents the physical, the head line represents the mental, and the heart line represents the emotional. Those are the basic energies or processes that make up our being. Any imbalance in the major lines shows an imbalance in the person and must be interpreted accordingly.

There are numerous configurations of lines, even for the major lines. They can run in all directions, and although there are directions that are common in most hands, as you read more hands, you will see the numerous routes that the lines can take. You should understand that lines are drawn to different areas of the palm because of the personality or physical structure of the person whose hands you are studying. If, for instance, a person has an intensely powerful sexual drive, this might produce a lack or weakness in another area, and because of the automatic balancing of these forces or energetic drives in themselves, people have different attitudes in life and different responses to life events. They develop different traits, different strengths and weaknesses.

The way to identify the beginning of a line is to find the thickest part of the line. The end of the line is where it tapers to a point. By understanding the quadrants and what they represent (see pages 27–40), you can understand the flow of any line. Its movement from one area to another shows you where energies are being taken. This gives you a personality profile for the person involved.

Whichever line you are looking at, you must look at the quality of that line. In the study of a line, remember:

- When looking at the line, ask yourself what impressions it gives of the psychological or physical quality it represents.
- Lines carry the flow of energy, and you must look at the quality of the line to see how the flow is carried.
- Look at the depth, consistency, and power of the line. This will give you an overall impression of the quality of the line itself and therefore some definition of the aspect of personality represented by the line.

- You need to consider whether the line is interrupted or whether it looks very direct and strong.
- Note any inconsistencies in the line, such as islands or fading or wavy lines.
- Examine lines that intersect or run from a major line, and consider the quadrant or other lines they run into.

## Broken Lines

Lines that are constantly broken obviously show breaks in the flow of energies of that line, and this must be taken into account.

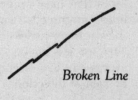

*Broken Line*

## Clear, and Straight Lines

A line that is drawn clearly and very straight shows a direct expression.

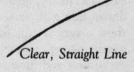

*Clear, Straight Line*

## Furred Lines

Furred-up lines show the slowing down of energy flow within that line.

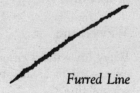

*Furred Line*

## Lightly Drawn Lines

Very lightly drawn lines depict a more conceptual and idealistic expression, less powerful and direct.

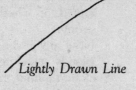

*Lightly Drawn Line*

## Many Connecting Lines off Main Lines

Lines that have numerous lines running off them show a frequent loss of energies, less direct expression, loss of energy by lack of direction.

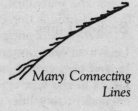

*Many Connecting Lines*

## Thick, Heavy Line

A thick, heavy, and deeply drawn line will obviously show a very strong and sturdy quality, a very basic expression and fundamental of that line.

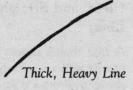

*Thick, Heavy Line*

## Wavy Line

Wavy lines show emotional expression or creativity and adaptability.

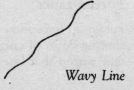

*Wavy Line*

## Subsidiary Lines

In his book *Chinese Hand Analysis*, Shifu Terence Dukes says, "Many of the so-called subsidiary lines reveal the passage of energies to and from the various quadrants. It is by observing these passages that we can determine the personal balance or lack of it within the individual, for they form a record of all the stabilizing actions taken within the mind/body organism within one's lifetime."

That is a good summation of the numerous lines that are neither major nor minor lines but show the transition of energies from one area of the palm to another, the drawing of resources from one particular area to balance another area of the palm.

It is worth repeating that to get a real insight into a person's hand, it is much better to get a good sense of the quadrants and the overall meaning of the major lines. Once this has been done, let your feeling of how these forces are interacting in the person's hand—how the lines are moving in relation to the quadrants and each other, and how the "subsidiary lines" are linking areas or connecting them—lead you to understanding.

# 8

## The Lifeline

The lifeline is one of the major lines. It is also called the vitality line, and in Chinese symbolism it is known as the major Earth line. The lifeline represents our physical expression and energies, and it represents our conscious expression of our physical energies within our lives.

This line begins about halfway between the base of the first finger and the base of the thumb. It sweeps around the ball of the thumb, terminating down toward the wrist.

### Reading the Lifeline

First of all, look at the quality of the lifeline. How do the energies seem to flow through that line? Is it drawn very strongly or lightly? A very heavily drawn lifeline shows very strong and solid expression of energies—often physical. A very lightly

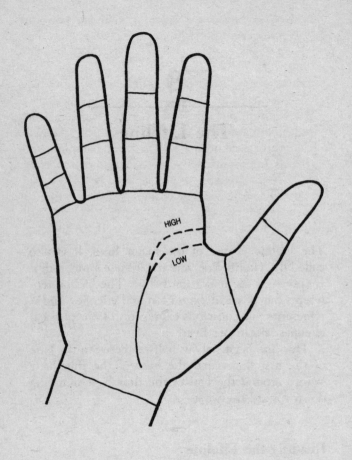

HIGH

LOW

*Lifeline—Height of Commencement*

drawn line is more subtle and refined, less powerful with more mental expression.

## Indications of Birth and Childhood

The beginning of this line tells us a lot about the influences inherited at birth and the physical strength or weakness of the person in early life, and so it is important to look closely at this starting point of the lifeline.

If the line is weak or broken at its start, then it shows possible illness or a lack of physical strength during early life. The commencement of any line obviously shows the quality of the root or source energies that flow through the line and show you on what sort of basis or foundation the line has been built. If the line looks damaged in early life, then try to find out from the person what caused the damage; there can be so many causes, but normally they are events in the physical or outer area of life. Then look at the line later in life to see what sort of recovery was made, what effect still remains. The line may be stronger or weaker. A weak start will affect the energies in the rest of the line because this is the root of the line.

## Starting High on the Hand

If the lifeline starts high on the hand—that is to say, it is closer to the first finger—this represents a person whose ambition is quite strong. He is someone who is physically quite active, but his expres-

sion is at a higher level than just physical. Perhaps
he is more of an aesthetic or mind-oriented person,
expansive and less limited in expression than many
people.

## Starting Low on the Hand

If the lifeline starts low on the hand, closer to the
base of the thumb, the person is more limited in
expression, being much more physical. These people will probably even look more earthy or physical,
and their activities will be more limited in the
sense of not including so much of the mental, artistic, or aesthetic.

## The Curvature of the Lifeline

Curvature of the lifeline is important. If the lifeline
curves well out into the hand and around the ball
of the thumb down toward the wrist, giving a
greater area within the lifeline, this shows strong
vitality. The wider the lifeline sweeps outward into
the middle of the palm, the more vitality is shown,
the more physically active the person will be,
whereas if the line drops very straight and almost
across into the ball of the thumb, leaving less area
of the palm within the lifeline, then this person
tends to be lacking in energy, not a very physical
person, not much of a physical presence, and his or
her physical energies are quite low. Obviously it is
important to balance what you observe of the ball
of the thumb with the quality of the lifeline. The

lifeline is encircling the ball of the thumb and is so dependant on the power that is seen in the ball of the thumb that whether it is well built or flat shows the sorts of energies, the very basic powerful energies that this lifeline is encompassing.

## Lines from the Lifeline

Branch lines running from the lifeline toward the mount of Lunar or the Water quadrant show a restless nature, a nature that is adventurous. The person will show a desire for change and stimulation.

These branches can be called a "wandering end." In some cases the lifeline itself may completely veer off into that direction. But more commonly there are branches coming off the lifeline toward the mount of Lunar.

People with these lines might find routine quite difficult to cope with. They seek stimulus and look for change in their lives and possibly for travel. In fact, these people are quite often travelers.

If these "wandering ends" become stronger than the original lifeline itself, this suggests the people may travel, not necessarily physically, but may make big changes in their social positions and in the circumstances from where they first began in life. Leaving behind the old or original ways of life may even become a motivation for them. Some palmists believe this means the subject may travel and not return to the home country. That is not necessarily true, but it does mean that in their search for movement in life these people may find

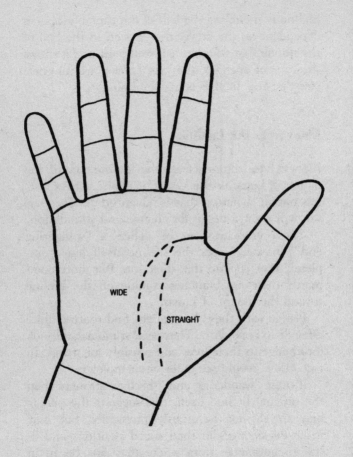

WIDE

STRAIGHT

*Lifeline—Curvature*

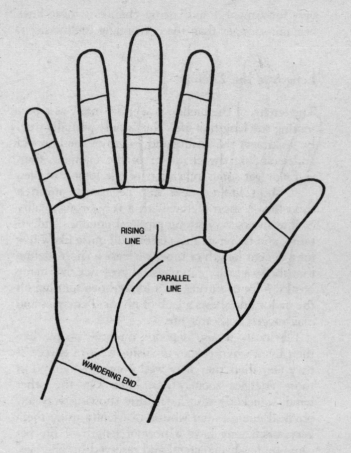

RISING
LINE

PARALLEL
LINE

WANDERING END

*Lifeline—Accessory Lines*

very fundamental and lasting change if these lines become stronger than the continuing lifeline itself.

## Length of the Lifeline

The length of the lifeline is seen by many as representing the length of life. This is only partially true. By looking at the quality and length of the line and understanding the character of the energies, then you may get some indication of the length of life.

A short lifeline does not necessarily mean a short life. A short lifeline with a very strong quality of line shows very strong physical energies and vitality, and therefore this person will quite likely live for a decent length of time, whereas a short lifeline that shows a lacking in physical presence, has many breaks, a lot of furring, or a lot of lines running off the major line shows a lack of physical energies and may suggest a shorter life.

Obviously it also depends on how people live their lives, whether they are using a lot of energy. If they are, then they may well come to the end of those energies sooner than later. On the other hand, somebody who has a line showing very few physical energies but who is not really using them very much may have a normal length of life because he has been careful and reserved his energies.

So it is a question of looking at the quality of the line, looking at the length of the line, and assessing how the person is using the energies to gauge the possible length of life. This is something that is learned with personal experience and judgment by observing the lifeline, and the more hands you see, the more you will be able to judge the length or strength of life.

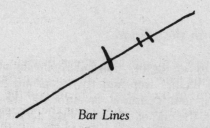

*Bar Lines*

## Bars on the Lifeline

Bars on the lifeline—that is to say, lines that run across the lifeline—are an interruption in the energy of the lifeline. They show times of stress and upheaval in the person's life depending on how strongly the bar crosses the lifeline.

These lines show the person is drawing on resources from within the lifeline, taking such resources to wherever the bar line terminates. Sometimes the bar lines can terminate on the head line or run across to the heart line or to different areas of the palm. If they terminate on the head line, it shows that the time of stress resulted in a lack of concentration and of the resources needed in the mental area. If the bar runs to the heart line, then it indicates emotional stress, a lack of emotional support, and subsequent emotional upheaval. Such times of stress obviously affect the flow of one's life and thus the lifeline. Such bars on the lifeline are quite common, and it is a good way of identifying major upheavals or periods of stress within a person's life.


## Breaks in the Lifeline

Breaks in the lifeline, particularly breaks where you see the lifeline stop and then continue beside or below it and continue on strongly, show major changes, the end of one part of the person's life and the beginning of the next. Usually very fundamental changes have occurred at such times. It can be illness resulting in great change, but more often, as I saw in one person's hand, it is something like marriage, which, being such a major alteration in a person's life, is shown as a very big break in the line.

If the end of one line and the beginning of the other run parallel to each other for a while, then good energy resources were, or will be, available during the change, and the period of change may occur over a number of years. Nevertheless the change is fundamental, but it does not represent a terminal condition, as some palmists may say.

Although the breaks show a major interruption to the physical energies, if the lifeline continues on strongly, then obviously there is a very positive conclusion to the major change. If the lifeline seems impaired after the break, then there have been lasting energy losses suffered in the change. If so, it would be helpful to the subjects if you can see strengths in their hands elsewhere and to point out how they may utilize such strengths. For instance, you may see potential in mental abilities or emotional energies. Quite often a lacking in one area is supplemented by more energies in another. If they are more emotionally or mentally powerful, encourage them to express these energies, and this in itself will often direct or release more energies physically.

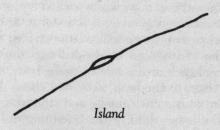

*Island*

## Islands in the Lifeline

Islands in the lifeline represent a division of the physical energies, a duality or dual expression of those energies, possible indecision, but certainly a weakening of the line. This is because the energies are split and are not concentrated or directed in one area.

An island is a bit like a branch line that is trying to expand into new expression, but instead of managing to establish a new direction it returns back to the lifeline. This only creates dispersion and division and depicts a period of weakening. It can also show physical weakness. Islands are generally caused by nervousness.

Chinese traditions in hand analysis state that islands usually relate to a mental and emotional period of duality, indecisiveness, or powerful external pressures. The difficulties are felt for the length of the island.

## The Three Areas of the Lifeline

To judge where a weakness caused by an island might occur in the body, it is useful to know how the lifeline has traditionally been divided into areas. The lifeline can be divided into three equal areas, and each area is related to the body. The top third relates to the head, neck, and chest; the middle third to the chest, lungs, and other thoracic organs; the lower third to the intestines and the reproductive organs. So where the island is located could suggest a weakness in that part of the body.

## Fine Lines Running off the Lifeline

Lots of fine lines running off the lifeline show a dispersion of physical energies in lots of different areas or directions. These people do not or cannot concentrate their endeavors or actions, but they are scattered in all sorts of areas. This frequently produces a waste of energies and a nervousness or disposition to anxiety which affects them physically.

## Striations in the Lifeline

Striations in the lifeline show lack of energy flow—a constant stopping and starting of energies. They may also depict difficulties in communication and

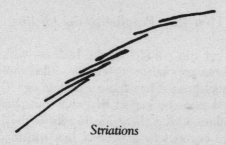

*Striations*

someone who does not feel at ease physically. This may lead to jerky movements, feeling ill at ease with the body, and possibly poor resistance to illness or a slowness to recover from illness.

## Rising Lines from the Lifeline

These represent changes in one's life but normally some sort of constructive change or some change that is to overcome a current situation. They show change from a current situation.

A rising line from the lifeline is identified by looking at the source of the line that is actually from the lifeline. That is the thicker end of the line, rising, and it then rises to a point at the other end. Such lines show excess energy leaving the lifeline. They can often be found when people take up secondary careers or get involved in study of some kind. They are usually trying to extend their lives in some way, doing something that requires a greater amount of energy and a certain amount of drive to make this creative change in their lives.

## Lines That Run Parallel to the Lifeline

Lines that run parallel to the lifeline—within the lifeline but parallel to it—can be called sister lines or parallel lines. They show a backup or secondary energy during the period that they run parallel to the lifeline. Often there are breaks in the lifeline that are covered by a parallel line within it, and these show an inner strength during a time of difficulty or change. The person is being helped or backed up by inner resources shown as the parallel line. This eases the pains of the change and provides greater energy resources. If there is no break in the line and there is also a parallel line, then that period can be quite powerful as far as energy resources are concerned and a constructive time for the person.

## Dots, Crosses, or Stars on the Lifeline

Dots are small marks on the line itself and often indented slightly. Sometimes if they are big, they can look like small pits. Dots show temporary illness by trapped or contained physical energies. Crosses on the lifeline mark sudden events caused by external forces. A star on the lifeline represents

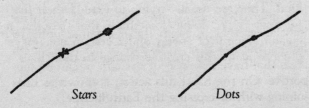

Stars                    Dots

a complete disruption in the energies of that time: a sudden event, a sudden explosion of energies, and an impact on a person's flow and direction.

## Lines Radiating from Within the Lifeline

The lines within the lifeline that run from the base of the thumb out toward the lifeline are lines carrying energy from that middle source out toward the lifeline. I tend to think of them as rays of sunlight or energy. If they are excessive, it shows excessive demands on those Earth or basic physical and psychological resources. If they are not excessive, it shows the normal flow of energy from the ball of the thumb containing the Earth energies.

## Plaiting or Crisscrossing of the Lifeline

This is often seen at the beginning of the lifeline and shows delicacy and vulnerability physically and possibly physical weakness or illness. Braided lines are another description of it.

## The Chinese View of the Earth/Lifeline

Our internal regulating process tends to deal with imbalances that occur in the body/mind unity by linking the needy or weak part of our beings with areas that have resources of strength or can be supportive. On the hand this action is shown as lines joining with or crossing the Earth/lifeline.

*Plaiting or Crisscrossing*

To understand what these lines are showing of internal processes, it helps to note where the line begins and moves to. If you realize that the beginning of the line gives it its power or influence and where it is moving to shows where that influence is being utilized or drawn on, then a clear insight into the process is gained. Therefore, if a line starts on the mount of Lunar and moves to the lifeline, it would suggest deep resources of creative imagination, instinctive or universal inner wisdom, are being called upon to support an action in the outward-going personality. One might even see what physical organs are influences by checking which organs of the body are connected with each area of the hand.

## Absence of the Earth/Lifeline

For a person not to have a lifeline is very rare. It does occur, however, and is usually connected with an excess of Air/mental activity and Fire/emotions. It can be brought about by temporary conditions of illness, great emotional stress, or extreme introversion, such as catatonia. The lack of the line shows that the flow of energies, such as those going into physical movement and mental and emotional response, has been slowed down to a minimum. It is like running a house on the very minimum of heating and lighting. This means the demarcation between the person and the environment is reduced. The person may lose much of the sense of self, even feeling as if he were slipping into unconsciousness or oceanic feelings—feelings of melting into an ocean of unconsciousness. Thus there may be an inclination to infection or being led by circumstances as the subject is largely in other people's hands. His survival is being handled only by the unconscious processes dealing with breathing, digestion, etc.

## An Intuitive Look at the Lifeline

This line is produced by the movement of the thumb across the palm or toward the other fingers. It is like a great wall, a great valley separating the hill that rises to the thumb. It can also be thought of as an enclosure within which is the domain or the castle of the ego or selfhood. Its shape, its sweeping curve are indicative of the power of the person's life and body, the power of selfhood as it exists in the material world.

Within this castle keep, this hold, are the fundamental powers of the body and personality, its health and confidence. This line does not particularly represent the actual length of life but has more to do with how strongly the personality exists within itself, the level of integration within the limited area of selfhood. It is the boundary, the strength that gives us separateness from other life-forms, other beings, and the environment. It is the dividing line between our own existence and the existence of other things. It is what enables us to say, "I exist as distinct from you."

Within each of us there is a strength or force, something that holds us together as a person, as a body. It is what makes the countless cells in the body work together. It is what leads the body to defend itself against attack—at a bacterial level and also at a personal level. That power is represented in the lifeline. That force or identity is not simply physical or psychological; it has to do with all levels of our being. It is this force that makes us exist as unique beings, protecting us from the environment and also motivating us to flourish in the environment.

If you look at the lifeline, if you see its shape, its form, its flow, its sweep, you see this immense power. It is the largest and most powerful line on the hand. It represents the foundations, the energy, the structure out of which the human being is made. It is the power of human life.

If a person's lifeline is weak or broken, it suggests the person is very vulnerable, not just emotionally but physically too. His identity has difficulty defending itself and surviving within all the forces, the energies that are life. Therefore, if the line is wide, strong, and long, it gives the impression that the person has the power to survive within the forces of life, within the environment, within social pressures. He can deal with the conflicts, the events, the threats and attacks that happen to all of us. At a physical level this could be seen as the immune system, which fights the attack of incoming bacteria and viruses. If it is weak, then the survival of the individual is uncertain. If it is strong, his survival is more sure and he does not appear to be fighting for life all the time. People with strong lifelines also have a good sense of separation, a good sense of selfhood.

If there are many breaks in a strong line, it doesn't necessarily say that the person is weak. The line itself is strong, even if it is broken at points. Breaks suggest these people will meet—perhaps through the way they are living—powerful counterforces, activities, or events that will threaten them or they will feel threatened by. If that happens, there is still enough strength in them to deal with that. They will press on despite setbacks.

If the line is weak, however, those counterforces, attacks, or events will be felt as much more threatening and will often deplete the person enormously. This is like an enemy's getting into the castle keep and running amok for a while. Even if the enemy is expelled, some damage has been done.

If the people don't have long lifelines, this doesn't necessarily mean they are not going to live very long. What it does suggest is that there is an enormous amount of power expended in a short period of time. The early parts of their lives flourish— a time when all their energy was expended—and their later lives have less energy in it. They have "done their thing" and flowered in the early years, and the flower fades quickly. This can of course influence the length of their lives. It may be that there is a withdrawal of energy. They may no longer flourish in the world or in their identity, so this might very well lead to an earlier finish of their lives or a withdrawal.

# 9

## The Head Line

The head line is also known as the line of the intellect, the mensal line, or, in the Chinese symbolism, the major Air line.

The head line represents intellect, reasoning ability, logic, and our consciousness. It doesn't necessarily represent how intelligent we are but the way we go about reasoning—the way we take in information and process it, the quality of the way we think or of our intellect.

## The Start of the Head Line

The head line normally starts close to or in the same position as the lifeline. This is between the base of the first finger and the base of the thumb. There are three basic positions in which the head line can commence:

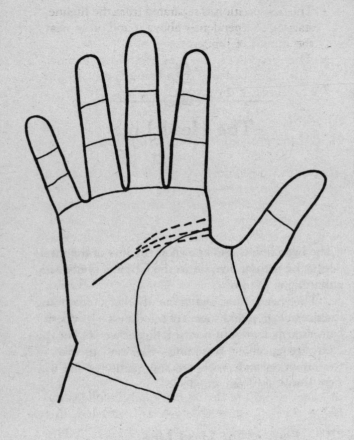

*Head Line—Height of Commencement*

- The first position is separated from the lifeline, starting independently above it and on or near the mount of Jupiter.
- The second position is as part of the lifeline.
- The third position is underneath and within the curve of the lifeline.

## Head Line Starting Above the Lifeline

The start of the head line independent of the lifeline and above it on the mount of Jupiter shows the subject is very independent in thought. It indicates independence from a very early age, and that the person has been independent from family influences from a very early age. The closer to the first finger or the higher the head line starts, the more independence is shown. If it is very high, it shows a certain degree of arrogance and overconfidence, foolhardiness, and the possibility of a great deal of belief in one's own attitudes and ideals.

It is important to remember any quality that goes too far becomes a weakness. For example, in this case the head line is separate from the lifeline, showing strong independence and individuality. But if the line starts too high on the hand, this independence may become arrogance and the person might lose touch with reality to some degree. This applies to all qualities in the hand. If they are extreme, they become a weakness.

## Head Line Starting Together with the Lifeline

The next position is where the head line starts with the lifeline. This is the most common position, and it shows a degree of cautiousness. It indicates an influence from the person's early environment and the family, and depending on how long the head and lifeline stay tied together, it shows the degree of influence on the person from the family and early life. If they are tied for quite a long time, then the influence is strong and the subject is a late developer as far as independence is concerned and ability for individual freethinking thoughts and attitudes.

If the head line is tied to the lifeline at its beginning but only for a short period, then it shows influence from family at an early age but also a good deal of independence. (The section on timing will help you understand and judge the period of influence and at what age independence was gained; see pages 232–39.)

## Head Line Starting Within the Curve of the Lifeline

This position shows overcautiousness, a very timid person, somebody who finds it difficult to think for himself and constantly needs to hear praises from others. It indicates someone who has a wish for stability and self-protection, perhaps in an extreme form, a person who is very dependent on family and home, country or religion. Nationalist, political, or racial views may be important to this person.

## End of the Head Line

The end of the head line is very important, and there are a number of places that it can finish.

### Head Line Ending in the Mount of Lunar

First, if it curves and terminates in the Water quadrant or the mount of Lunar, this shows a great deal of imagination in the thought process. If it curves very deeply into the Water quadrant or the mount of Lunar, it shows an overactive imagination, possibly losing touch with reality. This may produce some degree of depression depending on how that imagination manifests itself. But this depends on how much counterbalance is found in the rest of the hand.

So the head line falling very deeply into the Water quadrant or the mount of Lunar shows a very active imagination even to the extent of hallucination or something equivalent, and quite often it can result in depression.

The area of experience connected with the mount of Lunar is an area of ourselves that most are unfamiliar with and find difficult to cope with constructively. It holds in it a mass of experience gathered in the early stages of human evolution and,

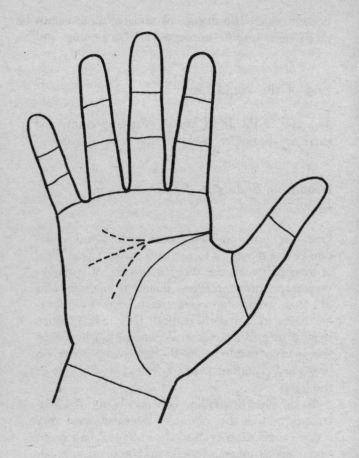

*Head line—Terminations*

although vastly important and useful, may not be integrated into the conscious personality and so may be felt as a threat or alien influence.

The head line that curves slightly into the mount of Lunar shows a balance between imagination and use of factual information and a practical approach in thought.

## Straight Head Line

A line that is very straight and runs right across the hand shows a lack of imaginative creativity. The person's decisions will be based more on factual information and an approach that assesses objectively what is thought or received as ideas. Ideas need to be proved to such a person. His or her views are very much either black or white.

## Forked Head Line

If the head line forks, and one fork runs to the mount of Lunar and the other fork runs across the hand, this can show a division and an inclusion of both imagination and practicality together. If one division is stronger than the other, then you can see which one is the dominant quality.

If a line forks from the head line or the head line itself curves up toward the top of the hand, toward the fingers, this shows an influence on the head line by the digit toward which the line is directed. Therefore, if the head line curves toward the little finger, then the mind would clearly be influenced and expressed in the area of communication and social interaction. And curving toward the ring finger would show an influence and expression with the person's creative energies and abilities.

### Rising Head Line

It is not common for the head line to rise, but when this occurs, it shows a certain loss of contact with reality. The person's ideas and thoughts may delusively seem very real and may thereby affect good judgment and actions in a negative way. The effect of the head line rising toward the fingers shows interests in the subjective, mental, and emotional experience of life instead of the physical. Such people may prefer their concepts of things instead of meeting things directly.

## Relationship Between Head Line and Heart Line

The other thing to look for is the relationship between the head line and the heart line or the Air line and the Water line. If the head line and the heart line are very close together, then this shows they have a great deal of influence on each other. Therefore thoughts would be very much influenced by the emotions. The Chinese symbolism of Air and Water suggests incompatibility. Therefore, if they are close together, this produces some sort of mental or emotional stress. The head line can sometimes run into the heart line, and this situation shows a much stronger union between the head and the heart and much stronger influence between them. These people can be greatly influenced by their emotions and thoughts, and a great deal of stress may be caused by this.

The farther apart they are, the more independent the mind is from the emotions and the greater the person's ability to make decisions without influence by the emotions.


## Merged Head and Heart Line

The line that is often misunderstood is the simian line. This occurs when, instead of two lines—the head and the heart line—there is in fact just one line where the head and the heart lines both fuse. In this case such people do not think rationally. They feel and react very strongly to their emotions and find it very difficult to separate thoughts from emotions. What they feel will be mistaken for thoughts and vice versa. This can also cause a great deal of stress and confusion in them.

The simian line exists only when the head and heart lines are fused together. Where a heart line exists that is completely independent from the head line and a second heart line fuses with the head line, this is not a true simian line. This is because the independent heart line creates a greater balance in the hand.

People with the simian line tend to throw themselves into whatever it is they are doing. Their emotions are very intertwined with their intellects, so they become very intense about anything they are involved in. They also find it difficult to know whether they think or feel their experiences.

The fusion of the head and heart lines to form a simian line can be seen in many different ways, but obviously the most intense form is where both the head and heart lines form one line only rather than two lines that fuse. Depending on the balance of the hand, it can work in a positive or negative manner. Some very prominent people have simian lines, and they have achieved great work because they have been so intense in carrying out their work. But there are also people with the marking who have carried out brutal crimes of passion.

## Characteristics of the Head Line

### A Deeply and Clearly Drawn Head Line

This indicates good energy flow, a good ability for thought and processing information. A deeply drawn line may denote strong values or philosophies that are not easily changed. A well-drawn, clearly defined head line shows high mental motivation and clarity, with a certain amount of fluidity in thought and attitudes.

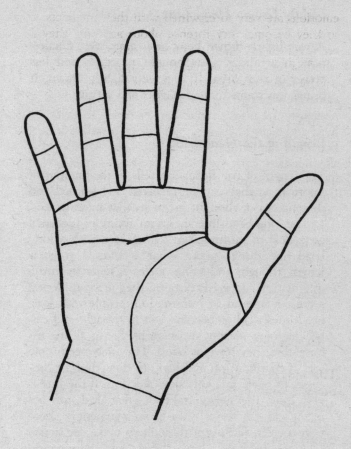

*Example of Simian Line*

## Lightly Drawn Head Line

A very lightly drawn head line shows more fluctuation in attitudes and thought processes and less power in that area. If it is very lightly drawn, it brings less stability in thoughts and attitudes.

## Length of the Head Line

The length of the head line tells us the amount of information that can be received and learned and the amount of thought given to that information.

The long head line shows an ability to process a great deal of information. The person with a long head line thinks about what is learned at great length, though, and so has a slower reaction to the information received. Because they are considering a greater amount of information, people with long head lines tend to become lost in thought and can become overcautious or oversensitive to all the information they have at hand. They may need some sort of coordination and logic to their thought processes to overcome this slow reaction. If the line is very long, the person takes a great deal into account and may see all sides to an argument or situation equally, finding it difficult to make decisions.

A short head line shows less information learned, less information processed, quicker reactions, and more logic. These people are very hasty but also logical and practical in the way they make their decisions, react very quickly, and don't tend to take much into account apart from the basic and obvious pieces of information. They need to develop a certain amount of patience, to be more thorough and should take more into account when making their decisions and in their thought processes.

Terence Duke suggests that the mental activity linked with the head line is like a TV antenna that picks up signals and that functions to produce images or concepts in our mind of what has been picked up. The mind then acts or reacts toward these images or concepts. The longer the line, the more signals are picked up and the more slowly their significance is realized. If the line is short, only a few signals are received and the images are quickly formed. The action indicated by long lines produces mental dispersion or indecision, and short lines tend toward triviality. The longer line requires more discipline to act in a way linked with information received.

## Breaks in the Head Line

If a break is found causing the head line to stop and recommence elsewhere, this shows a new direction, possibly a new start in the person's attitudes and thoughts. The person meets a new beginning psychologically. Although it often takes a lot of energy and courage to make such a change, it is usually a good thing as long as the line continues strongly afterward. Where the line breaks but there is an overlap, it shows a period of time over which the change has taken place. During that period there will be a dual attitude or a duality. When there is no overlapping, there could be more of a sudden

change and more of a clean break from old
thoughts and attitudes.

## Bars, Fuzziness, Striations, or Islands on the Head Line

Bars, which are short lines, crossing the head line
show an interruption in the energy flow of the head
line. Fuzziness or furring in the head line shows
slowing down of energies in the mind, interruptions
in the clarity of thought, and a lacking in sharpness
of thought.

Striations in the head line show a lack of concentration and a lack of continuity and flow
through the head line. A certain amount of mental
stress is caused as a result. Islands on the head line
show periods of stress. Islands indicate an inability
to break out or change attitudes and often occur
during times of mental stress. These islands can
often appear for a brief period and later disappear.

Often you find islands on the head line that occur at about the same time as markings on either
the heart line or lifeline. This shows either physical
or emotional problems have had their effects on
feelings as well as the mind.

## Dots or Stars on the Head Line

Dots or stars found on the head line show a sudden
shock to the mental system and could indicate illness over the period of disturbed energies.

## Many Fine Lines Leaving the Head Line

Lots of fine lines leaving the head line show worry and a loss of force from that line. It indicates a concern over small things and that the person lacks the ability to direct his or her mental energies.

The subsidiary lines that cross the head line, such as the lines that are running from one quadrant to the next, from one part of the palm to another, should first be looked at to see where the line is running from and to. By looking at the subsidiary line and understanding the area it moves to, you will then have an indication of the cause of the interruption to the head line.

## An Intuitive Look at the Head Line

An intuitive investigation of this line leads to a feeling that it has never ever really been understood. It has been called the head line. It has been connected with the way people think or their mental lives, and that isn't really correct. It has to do with understanding.

There is in each of us a process that has to do with responding to the environment. The heart line has to do with relationships and how people connect with one another, but the head line emerges from something else that happens in life. If I say that everybody has an ability of some sort— like a skill in knowing the way, or a skill in making a table, or a skill in talking to other people—this line represents that type of skill. It has to do with skills that people develop or that are sometimes apparently innate in themselves.

If I ask people what they do, they usually talk about what their activities are, what their work is, what they are interested in. But if I ask who they are, it produces quite a different effect. They might respond in terms of how they feel or how they see themselves, their likes and dislikes, and so on.

The head line stands somewhere between these two areas of the person's life. It expresses what tendencies a person has or what sense of self a person develops. It deals with the interlinked groups of ideas and feelings people have about themselves. It also describes in its strength or configurations what they do with their self-images, what they develop in the world from or with the views they have of life, of themselves, of the physical world. It describes their potential to create from this side of themselves in terms of their activities. It connects with the techniques they use to interact with other people and the environment. So one could easily call this the life-skill line.

To understand this point, it helps to think of early human beings and consider how they learned to see the connection between their needs and the natural resources around them. From this they developed certain skills such as weaving and pottery making. Such abilities did not arise necessarily through careful reasoning, but by recognizing, perhaps unconsciously at first, how things would work, how they would fit together, how they would combine and influence one another. This is not the same as planned rational thought, although we still have this skill of understanding the nature of things in abundance. This skill can apply to anything: seeing how people will conflict or harmonize in work, finding what is wrong with a car by listening to it, solving a problem by jumping out of the lines of rational thought that only suggested answers that did not work, and so on. So apart from this being called the life-skill line, it could be called the intelligence line, if intelligence is defined as shrewdness, perception, being able to vary one's behavior in response to varying situations and requirements.

If a person has not developed certain life skills, this line in itself will appear to be weak. It will not be as deeply founded as it would if the person has involved himself in taking hold of abilities that enable him to manipulate things, to change things in the world. If the line is deep and well formed, it suggests the person has the capability to develop social and manipulative skills.

In looking intuitively at how this line came into being, one can see it has a connection with the ape's hand. It is obviously connected with the single simian line (see pages 159–61) across the palm, but it has a difference in that it develops; it leaves its strict line across the palm and shifts down, sometimes to the lower region of the hand. This wasn't so originally, and the reason for the change was that in the past human beings had to learn to manipulate gradually not only the external world but their own inner feelings, much more fully than the apes. They had to learn to walk in between the outside world and their own inner lives. Consciousness brought with it such difficulty. The struggle became much more than other creatures faced. They met difficulties that other creatures have never faced. They had to learn to handle their feelings in a similar way to learning the skill to wield a piece of wood. If this had not been possible, humans would not have learned to control their appetites enough to plant seed or their urges sufficiently to live together as peaceably as they manage to do. Without conscious control they would have eaten the harvest they were growing instead of storing it. Somehow they learned to hold back on certain aspects of themselves. Over and over again, following taboos and religious beliefs enforced by punishment, they reminded themselves to manipulate their own emotions and thoughts.

What hasn't been said about this line in the past is that if a person has a line that includes smaller lines running parallel with it, this suggests he or she has a multitude of skills. His or her life has a tendency to flow or endeavor meaningfully in a number of ways.

If a person has a line that leans toward the larger area of the "percussion" side of the hand, this relates to the unseen or the irrational aspects of the self that may lead to madness or despair. But there is another side to this because it says many of that person's skills have to do with manipulating the inner life or are connected with the inner life. It may not mean these people become despairing or despondent. What it does suggest is that a lot of their attention, their feelings, and their external functions are more fully involved in the urges and drives within that humans struggled to control and push beneath consciousness. For instance, people suffering depression have their attention so focused on painful or despairing emotions, they are not capable of dynamic relationships with others or events.

If a hand has a very shallow or small head line, this suggests the person's intellect is not very well refined or developed. This has nothing to do with not being intelligent. It simply suggests such people haven't applied or pitted themselves or their wits against events and their environment. Their skills have not developed. Their intelligence hasn't been used, taken up, and applied to develop skills that might be used in manipulating the world or changing their external lives.

Something that is often present in a hand is a certain type of mark on the head line. It is almost like a crater or a depression, a sort of weakness in the line. It gives the impression of immense energy that's drained away. It is not that the people haven't got motivation or haven't had energy, but something happened in their lives at that point that has almost destroyed them. They survive, but at that point their self-images were devastated and had to be rebuilt.

When the head line is linked with the lifeline in the early part of the line, this has a meaning that has often been stated as connecting the person with others, making him dependent. If you consider this line is about skill rather than about mind and intellect, then it can have a slightly different interpretation. It implies that in the early stages of personal growth these people were influenced by others in the direction they took in developing their social and work skills and only gradually developed their own initiatives in these areas.

If the line stands by itself, it suggests those people found it difficult to absorb from others, to link their lives with others. Although they may have developed skills, this may have been difficult for them. Also a separate head line sometimes suggests people leaving something behind, being able to leave behind attitudes and emotions that were very prevalent in their early lives, as if they were capable of doing that and standing apart from their beliefs.

# 10

## The Heart Line

The heart line, also known as the line of love in Chinese symbolism, is the major Water line. The major Water line represents our emotions, our emotional consciousness, our ability to love, and the range of emotions that are available to us. It also covers such things as intuition and spiritual wisdom. This line always starts in the same position. It is the only one of the major lines that always starts in the same position: in the Air quadrant below the little finger.

According to Dukes, in *Chinese Hand Analysis*, "The water line always begins in the same general area, this in itself is a remarkable feature for it shows certain forms of experience are always governed or set according to inviolate principles. Since water relates to emotional experience it reveals a pattern to which all human kind is subject."

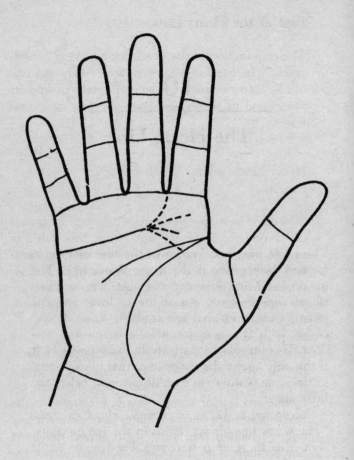

*Heart Line—Terminations*

## End of the Heart Line

The termination of the heart line can vary considerably. The heart line can terminate below any one of the fingers, but in general it tends to find its place, find its end, underneath the first or second finger.

### Heart Line Ending Under the First Finger

When the heart line terminates high on the mount of Jupiter, just below the first finger, this indicates people who have very highly developed emotions and have a great deal of expectations in their emotions. They are the type of people who will be very devoted to their partners or within marriage tending to put their partners on a pedestal. They can easily be disappointed in love but tend to be very faithful within a relationship or marriage. They have a tendency to follow a leader figure or join a religious group. This line ending here shows an excessive amount of Water. This is because it is the major Water line and terminates just below the first finger, which is the Water digit. When the heart line terminates on the mount of Jupiter or just below it, this gives a very long heart line, which increases even more the range of emotions available to the person. It shows a very highly emotional and sensitive person with a great deal of feeling expression. These people can be motivated almost entirely by their emotions and gain great drive to do things if their emotions are stimulated in the right way. But their emotions can also work in the opposite way and be destructive, so these people can tend to be quite moody and fluctuate from one emotion to another quite easily.

## Heart Line Ending Between the First and Second Fingers

When the heart line terminates between the first and second fingers, curving up to the top of the hand, this is the most common position and is the most healthy and balanced termination of the heart line. The heart line is close to the first finger, which is the Water finger. This causes sensitivity to the line and adds far greater emotional expression, together with the practicality of the Earth finger.

## Heart Line Ending Under the Second Finger

When the heart line terminates underneath the second finger, which is actually the Earth digit, it represents physically expressive emotions. This is because the line is shortened, and that limits the range of emotions available to the person. The person with the heart line ending here is more likely to be emotionally cautious and have a high level of sensuality. He or she may also be attracted by the physical and by physical stimulation.

## Heart Line Ending near the Lifeline

When the heart line terminates very close to the lifeline, crossing the head line in doing so, this shows a very physically expressive kind of person. These are people who like to touch, people who like physical declaration within love, and who like a lot of physical contact with others.

This ending is inhibitive in some ways because the emotions need to be expressed so physically, inhibiting the person from other forms of experience. If the end of the heart line is actually within the circle of the lifeline, then there is an even greater need for physical expression, and often these people may have a hypersexual drive or have some sort of sexual deviancy. This characteristic can give a masculine expression to a female's hands or a feminine sensitivity to a male's hands.

Endings near or within the circle of the lifeline are quite unusual. This person certainly has a very different expression emotionally and sexually.

## The Heart Line Ending Above the Head Line

If the heart line terminates above the head or Air line or near the head line, or even on the head line, this shows the person's feelings are deeply influenced by his thoughts. Therefore this person tends to think rather than feel, and his emotions tend to be inhibited by thoughts or by the thinking processes. This can be useful in controlling emotions but restrictive within the person's emotional life.

## Heart Line Influenced by the Fingers

The heart line is influenced by the qualities of whichever finger it terminates beneath or is attracted toward. If the heart line terminates below the first finger, which represents the Water quality, then that person tends to be very emotional, very sensitive, with very highly developed emotions. If it ends under the Earth finger or in very rare cases under the Fire finger, then it is influenced by the qualities of those fingers.

# Characteristics of the Heart Line

## Curving Heart Line

A heart line that curves shows sensitivity. The normal heart line has a moon shape as it curves up between the second and the first finger. So curvature of any degree adds sensitivity. A heart line that has very little curvature or is completely straight has little sensitivity and shows directness of expression of emotional energies. People with a straight line shape may have no subtlety to their emotional expression and be strong and direct about their needs.

## Strongly Drawn Heart Line

A thick, clear, well-drawn heart line, deeply marked, shows strong emotional energies and very stable, solid expression. A well-drawn line shows more fluidity or adaptability to the emotional energies.

### Lightly Drawn Heart Line

A very lightly drawn line shows a lack in emotional energies and instability. The person is an emotional lightweight.

### Chained or Plaited Heart Line

Lines that are chained or plaited show emotional disharmony, restricted expression, disturbed energy flow. These people may be very emotional and lacking directness.

### Bar Lines, Stars, and Islands Across the Heart Line

Bar lines and stars across the heart line show shocks to the emotional system and emotional stress. Islands on the heart line again show a weakness emotionally or a period of emotional stress or weakness.

### Breaks in the Heart Line

If there are breaks in the heart line, it shows a change in the person's emotional life, the ending of one expression, way of life and a beginning of another. This may refer to the ending of a relationship. If the break overlaps, then this can be over a period of time; if there is no overlap, then this can be quite a sudden change.

## Branches Off the Heart Line

Branches off the heart line show a seeking of energies from wherever the branch runs. For example, if a branch runs into the Earth quadrant, then this will add physical expressiveness to the emotions.

## Doubled Heart Line

If there is more than one heart line, then this greatly increases the emotional energies of the subjects and greatly increases the range of emotions available to them. It shows a great deal of receptivity and sensitivity toward intuition and spiritual wisdom, depending on which line is stronger or dominant. If the upper line is stronger, then the emotions are expressed more conceptually, and if the lower line is stronger, then this person has a more physical expression. Nevertheless with two lines there is much more emotional energy and much greater emotional complexity, and by carefully studying which way the lines run, you will be able to determine the emotional expression of the person.

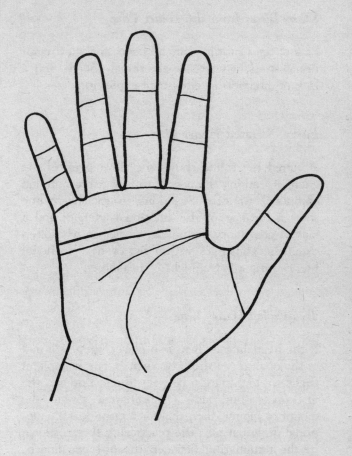

*Heart Line—Doubled Line*

## Many Lines from the Heart Line

Lots of lines running off the heart line show emotional stress, a waste of emotional energy, and a lack of direction in emotional expression.

## Furry, Striated Heart Line

A furred heart line shows the slowing up of the energies, causing the person to lack expression and emotional warmth. Striations in the heart line show a breakup of the emotional energies and a lack of continuity. It indicates a person who often experiences changes within his or her emotional life, causing a fair amount of instability.

## Two-Ended Heart Line

If the heart line ends in two places, there is a mix of the qualities of those two places. For example, if there is a termination between the second and the first fingers and also a termination toward the mount of Jupiter, then there is a great deal of emotional drive but also the practicality that is shown by the termination between the first two fingers. There is a duality in the emotional expression, depending on which line is stronger. The stronger line is dominant in expression, and the other line is similar to a branch, fulfilling a need or a lack.

The longer the heart line, the greater the range of emotions available to the person, and the shorter the line, the more basic and more limited the range of emotions available.

## An Intuitive Look at the Heart Line

There is so much here to grasp and pull together, so much that humans can learn about themselves. This line is not just about our personal lives now but also about human evolution, about how we came to be, how we are. It involves all of these and shows too how humans expressed themselves differently from other creatures.

The line deals with how people connect, how they relate, how they live their lives together, whether their lives actually connect with other people, whether they are independent, lonely, whether there are factors in their lives that create difficulties. It concerns how we open ourselves to the connection that exists between us and other human beings.

If this line has clear direct curves, if it lifts in a well-formed curve as it crosses the hand, this says these people's lives, emotions, and thoughts predispose them to trust other people, to allow other people to share something with them, to work with them, to make some sort of connection. The connection made is not simply a social meeting but links them in ways of work, of endeavors, of sharing, of responsibility.

Sexuality is one of the ways we connect with other people, we link our lives with theirs. Although this line is not particularly about sexuality, it does relate to sexuality in that if a person can't allow other people into his life more fully than a physical connection, then sexuality will be his means of connecting. But the heart line isn't principally about sexuality. It is about whether someone can let another person make a connection with him beyond his defenses and fears, within his vulnerable intimacy. If a car has a towing bar on it, it makes a connection with another vehicle like a van, towing it along. What one of the vehicles does influences the other. When we really connect with another person, it is very much like this.

So if this line is malformed, it expresses certain traits in a character that make it difficult for these people to make direct connections with other people. They would often feel themselves threatened or frightened of being abused or hurt. They often lack a clear sense of themselves in relationship with other people. We can think of this like the way we feed birds. We put food out and then we go away and the birds come and eat the food. This is the way some people live their lives. For them there has to be a disconnection. They do not like the direct contact.

In a few people the heart line may even dip down toward the wrist, and this really shows a person some or most of whose energies are internalized. Such people's affections are turned away from other people, and they may become recluses, trying to avoid contact with other human beings altogether.

On some people's hands the heart line does not have a continuous sweep. It is often bent or tangled. This depicts the struggles, the difficulties, the reservations, perhaps even the pains these people face in relation to other human beings. Somewhere in the life and development of these people their feeling connection with others has been deeply disturbed or their trust broken by betrayal.

If a person has a heart line that has a plain, smooth curve, but there is a kink in it, we could say here is a person who is newly formed, fresh minted. Such people have had neither good nor bad experiences of human beings; thus the virginal quality of the line. On the smooth part of the line there is nothing that has turned them away from nature. They only turn toward it. They have their own desires, their wants, and they move toward these as naturally as a horse to water. But if they have been injured, been beaten, been kicked, been pushed, or their inner harmony has been disturbed in some way, then that inclination toward others, toward the world, toward fulfillment and contact has been damaged, has been twisted. Thus the bent line.

When you look at this line and part of the hand and they are strong and rich, this isn't a sign that the person hasn't had trouble. It is the line of somebody who has met many ills and has found a way through them. Such people have the ability to find their way through these difficulties and can still make deep connections with other people. They have created in themselves, through facing and overcoming their own pain, what we call love. Their being is open, willing to receive what is true in another human being.

The heart line deals with an intensely important area of ourselves, because human beings spend most of their lives relating to other human beings. It is of prime importance in work as well as love relationships. It is not true that love has only to do with male and female relationships. It is part of all the connections we make with the external world. It has to do with all the ways we relate to society, to the forces that govern us, to those who extend to us, even to the way we relate to knowledge.

Therefore, in considering this line carefully and helping people to understand and use this side of themselves, we can radically change their lives. If they can understand the factors that stand in the way of their integrating with the world around them and therefore finding more satisfaction, their whole lives could change.

If the heart line extends around the percussion edge of the palm, it suggests the person has roots that go deep, roots that extend far and wide. Such people's connections with society through their families, through their pasts, are very strong. They have a lot of connections with other people in the world that are already in place. This is something they can build upon. If the line from there on is breached, then they haven't in fact developed those qualities. They have not built upon those connections. When a heart line with strong roots is jumbled and bent, then those connections haven't been made use of.

The line occasionally swings lower after leaving the percussion edge. If, after coming away from the edge of the hand, it doesn't glide upward but dips, this dropping, this falling line gives to the person a tendency to pull back. They may show great suspicion, which manifests itself in a feeling that if people really show the world who they are, they will not be accepted. They have a sense of care or caution about how they express themselves, how they show themselves to the world. Such people could be quite guarded in revealing themselves, what they want, who they are, and in fact create a suspicion in other people of not really knowing them. People may not trust them fully. They might become lonely, having difficulty in finding others who allow them into their lives easily. Because of these difficulties, they might believe there is no friendship in life for them.

The heart line is partly a buffer line. In early human beings it was a line that broke away from the simian line. If we take the simian line, the straight line across the hand, as a base line, this line is lifted from it. There was a change, something happened in the shape of the hand, in the way the hand was used. The change had to do with how the thumb and small finger can meet and how the hands relate to that movement. The fingers can curve; the small fingers can curve over toward the thumb, can meet and enfold the thumb. This took a long time to happen. The movement came about because human beings tried to alleviate problems of survival and to create a way of life that had less uncertainty in it. They wanted to be more in control of their own environment, to be able to stop certain things from happening and to produce other things. In doing so, they started manipulating objects, creating things, making things with their hands, and it was out of these long periods of change and creativity that the hands developed the movements that we now take for granted. Thus this line came about from actually trying to control the environment.

This is an oversimplified explanation of the development of the heart line, but this line has in it this history, this heritage, this change in human life. How this connects with relationships is that at some point human beings no longer wanted simply to receive of the environment; they no longer wanted simply to take what arose from their surroundings and tolerate them or just survive. They began to act upon their environment much more fully. They began to develop a two-way relationship with it, and this line, in its depth, expresses something of the way human beings relate to their environment. Part of this environment, sometimes a dangerous part, but always an important part, is other human beings. Because of this, there gradually arose the refinements of relationship. The enormous possibilities of relationship—in terms of not only person to person, but also person to world, person to work, person to self—were felt and developed.

When we look at the heart line, we see that any line that descends from it toward the wrist represents energy that interiorizes. It is energy that turns back inward, but also energy that connects the inner world of the person with his relationships. So the lines descending may show people who in their relationships are far more aware of their own internal feeling responses to what is going on externally. If there are no descending lines, the people may be very or totally unaware of their internal responses to their relationships with the world.

Rising lines are in a way the opposite of descending lines. They show what those people have contributed to others or to the world. It is something they have given of themselves. In a way the line can be dated in a similar way to the lifeline, and at times the people may have transcended themselves, given themselves in such a manner that it has left a mark on the hand.

On the male hand the line occasionally reaches toward the thumb farther before it rises. This is less frequent in the female hand, and this has to do with attributes that have been developed in the male personality. It comes about from a long period of time using the discipline of curtailing oneself, holding oneself back, being active in the world but with caution. If this movement to the thumb is very pronounced, it would mean the person has attained a shrewd caution. It can be likened to walking through a jungle and being aware that there are creatures around that could be dangerous. So people with this line may contain their exuberance or their laughter. Or they are hunters, and so they hold, they discipline, they contain their natural responses. They are people with not so much caution as a great deal of care in how they express themselves in the world. These people might well be diplomats or some kind of politician, certainly those who could be go-betweens in difficult situations.

# 11

## The Fate or Destiny Line

The destiny or fate line is known as the minor Earth line in Chinese elemental symbolism. Generally it runs from the bottom of the hand, above the wrist, and rises to the top of the palm and the fingers. This is from the passive area of the palm, up into the active area of the palm.

The fate line exists in many different forms and has various beginnings as well as endings. The line represents stability and balance within the person as well as indicates the degree of individual drive and direction within the person.

## No Fate Line

The fate line is not always present in the hand and is quite often found to be completely absent. The people without fate lines tend to be less predictable, to dislike routine and will be inclined not to plan their lives very much. They like to allow external forces to maneuver or affect their lives more than a person with a fate line. People without fate lines are less dependable and, I would say, have a tendency toward more restlessness and more change within their lives.

## With a Fate Line

The presence of a fate line indicates drive, inner direction, and a degree of planning in a person's life. There is more balance, reliability, and a certain amount of routine found in the activities of the person. It denotes the possibility of the person's settling down. But certainly the presence of a fate line shows the individual's decision to take control of the direction of his or her life.

## End of the Fate Line

### Fate Line Stopped Halfway

It is also important where the line stops. If the line rises on the lower palm but stops halfway up the hand, the early life of the person may have been well planned and directed and the later life less so. Generally it shows a strong start in direction and career and then a more unpredictable or more aimless end.

## Fate Line Stops at the Heart Line

If the fate line is visibly stopped or weakened by the heart line, there may be a restriction to the direction the person takes by emotional fears, loves, etc. The direction may be sacrificed for a relationship or for emotional expression.

## Fate Line Stops at the Head Line

If the fate line is visibly stopped or weakened by the head line, there is the possibility of people's directions being restricted by their own ideas and thought processes. For instance, people with great talent might believe that they have no skills or have failed in life. Or they might think a good direction for them would be a safe one rather than one they love.

## Fate Line Stopped by Other Lines

Other subsidiary lines that may visibly stop or bar the fate line again show the interruption and disturbance of that direction within the person by whatever the subsidiary line represents.

# Starting Positions of the Fate Line

The fate line can start in a number of places. It can start from the middle of the palm just above the wrist and rise to the top of the palm. This start position shows a balance between the unconscious and conscious quadrants, a balance between the practical and imaginative drive, a balance among family, restrictive influence, and an external, more liberated influence, a balance between more conventional and less conventional directions.

The beginning of this line shows where the person's drive and motivation has started from. The ending of the line shows where or how the person expresses his or her drive.

## Fate Line Starting from the Lifeline

If the fate line commences on the lifeline or within the lifeline, there is a very strong influence from the family, from early life, on the direction the person takes. It shows a certain degree of conventionalism, a degree of cautiousness, but also a high degree of stability. These characteristics are greater the farther the line commences from within the lifeline.

## Fate Line Starting from the Mount of Lunar

If the fate line starts from within the mount of Lunar, this shows a more imaginative and independent commencement to the person's direction. Here is a person who is more dependent on an audience. Such people want others around them in what they do and in what they achieve. They are

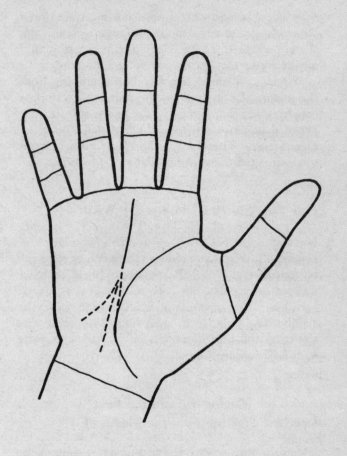

Fate Line—Place of Commencement

the type of person who chooses a less conventional direction. Because the mount of Lunar is within the Water quadrant, it adds creativity, imagination, and sensitivity to the person's drive and direction.

It seems to me that a fate line beginning from the mount of Lunar shows the start of direction in people's lives that has come from deep within their personal creativity—from their dreams or their imaginations. They have a more fanciful or a more inner-directed conception of their path in life.

## Fate Line Starting Close to the Wrist

It is important how high on the palm the fate line begins. If it starts very close to the wrist, at the very bottom of the palm, the person is likely to have decided on a particular path or direction at a very early age. These people usually manage to achieve a stability and balance in their lives. The higher on the hand the line starts, the later in life this path and direction are found.

## Fate Line Moving Toward the First Finger

If the line runs toward the first finger, it shows very powerful people who will not easily give up on what they are aiming for. They have a strong ambition and a strong desire to achieve.

### Fate Line Moving Toward the Second Finger

If the fate line runs toward the second finger, it indicates these people are more conventional in their expression. They are likely to enter into business and live in a responsible and conventional manner.

### Fate Line Moving Toward the Third Finger

If the fate line runs toward the third or ring finger, the person has a motivation to express himself or herself creatively and artistically.

### Fate Line Moving Toward the Fourth Finger

The fate line rarely runs toward the fourth finger, but if it does, this person will have an attraction to communication and the media and may need social or public acceptance.

### More than One Fate Line

This indicates two directions, two paths within these people's lives. Possibly they will have an inclination toward having two careers, two major directions in their life, both of them important. The two lines may start from different positions, have different endings and also different qualities, and therefore show different facets of the person.

## Characteristics of the Fate Line

### Length and Strength of the Fate Line

From the strength and length of this line we can see the degree of stability or even restriction within the person. It's a bit like the track of a railway: Depending on how long and clear the line is, it shows how far that person will take that route and will be less open to other routes or ways and more directive in his or her path in life.

The longer the line is, the more powerful its qualities are; the shorter the line, the less powerful. Many hand analysis books say that if the fate line is long and strong, then people will find success in life because of their strong and complete expression and direction in life. They might never become famous or rich, but they will, in their own sphere, achieve and feel successful. However, it should be kept in mind that success in life is not always as society sees it. The strong fate line indicates success as far as the person sees it. Therefore a very long and strong line can often be found in people who are not immediately seen as successful but who may have found a lifestyle they are content with and within which they find a good expression and balance in their lives.

## Thick, Well-Drawn Fate Line

A heavily drawn line shows people who take a direction with great force and motivation. They remain stable and committed to their direction but are perhaps lacking flexibility and are more staid. A well-drawn fate line shows more flexibility and balance, despite their energetic approach. People with very heavily drawn and strong fate lines dislike change, are often set in their ways, and remain conventional.

## Lightly Drawn Fate Line

This is an indication of slightly "laid-back" people, with less powerful motivation. They have greater flexibility, are less stable, and have more conceptual and idealistic direction.

## Broken Fate Line

This means the fate line will end, then start again. There are likely to be major changes in the person's direction and balance. If the break overlaps, then this could occur over a period of time. If there is no overlap in the break, then the change is more sudden and immediate.

## Striations or Frequent Breaks in the Fate Line

Frequent changes of circumstances and "changes of heart" are a part of this person's experience. Because of this, he or she lacks a real sense of continuity. Nevertheless a degree of direction and balance is still maintained.

## Islands, Dots, or Bars on the Fate Line

Islands indicate periods of weakness in these people's direction and balance. They feel a duality or split in themselves, and this results in indecision or distraction. Dots on the fate line show more sudden interruptions and shocks to the balance. Bar lines across the fate line reveal interruptions, normally caused by stressful situations in the person's life.

## Lines Joining the Fate Line

Branches connecting to the fate line represent energies and qualities supplementing the fate line from the area of the palm from which the branch has come. For instance, a line from the mount of Lunar would indicate supportive, imaginative, or creative ideas.

## An Intuitive Look at the Fate Line

This is a very powerful line. It carries with it energies from deep within the being. Whereas the life-line flows around a certain area, like a wall, this line is flowing right from the body directly up the hand. It is a line that balances. It is a flow between opposing forces—the great power of the thumb and the muscle at its base, and the power of the percussion side, the mount of Lunar and its great muscle there. It is the line that divides or balances those two forces, the two sides of the hand, the conscious and unconscious, the internal and external.

This line is something like a charioteer who is controlling a number of horses. They could easily pull in different directions and so get nowhere. Instead this line flows right up the hand, depicting the power of people not only to balance the forces within themselves but also to meet external pressures and forces, challenges, events, social pressures, condemnation, praise—to meet all these things and find a way to continue the journey of life, to continue this expression of themselves.

This line has to do not so much with fate—as if the personality were going to do or become something despite itself—as with destiny, with what is inherent or innate within the person and can be or is allowed to flower. So such people are not becoming something despite themselves but because of themselves. It is about materializing, making real in the world, what is at the heart of the person, his spirit.

This line therefore has to do with self-realization, with becoming ourselves despite not only the internal fears, hopes, and sexual drives we have but also the external pressures and events of life. It is about the force to carry on despite these, or perhaps even through using these in a process of self-realization and self-expression.

In many lives, people are buffeted this way and that by the forces of their fears, their lack of any sense of self-worth, and external factors, and if so, they may lack determination and a fate line. But if they in some measure realize themselves in the world despite such buffeting, then this line is a sign of that power.

If the line is not a long one, this does not mean the person is not very fully self-realized. However, sometimes it stops at the head or the heart line, and this suggests that within such people there are thoughts, self-doubts, or emotions that prevent a fuller expression of themselves. There are determining factors within themselves that do not allow them to go as fully into the outside world as they could do without those factors.

If I look at this line, which is better called the line of destiny, I have a sense of something flowering, of something opening up. There is a feeling of something that wasn't there before realizing itself, and that has to do with the person's life, that at one period didn't exist but has come about and opens and realizes itself and is known in the world. This is a good image of this line.

If this line has a tendency toward the first or second finger, this indicates the realization of the person is closer to a manifestation of himself in a physical sense, such as manufacturing goods or the creation of something that is physically apparent. If the line has a tendency toward the third or fourth finger, it suggests the person tends to express himself more in the direction of abstract ideas, music, the arts. His communication is in a less materialistic form.

# 12

## The Secondary Lines

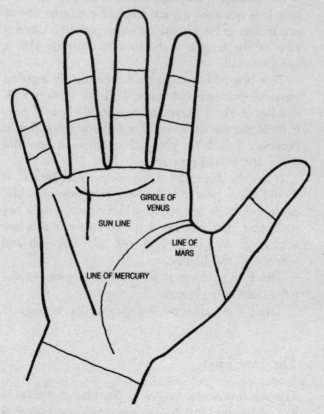

GIRDLE OF
VENUS

SUN LINE

LINE OF
MARS

LINE OF MERCURY

*Secondary Lines*

## The Line of Mars

The line of Mars, or the Chinese major Fire line, starts parallel with the lifeline and within the curve of the lifeline. It can also start joined with the lifeline. It is normally quite a short line, maybe one or two inches in length, but in some people it can run most of the length of the lifeline although this is quite unusual.

This line adds vitality to the person. It supports physical strength and spirit, and the person with this line is likely to recover very easily from illness. It gives the person more of a fighting spirit that is expressed mostly in physical strength, a powerful build, and sexual potency.

It has also been called the temper line because it is said these people have fiery temperaments and easily lose their temper or self-control. This is not really true. The fundamental expression of this line is physical and in general just adds strength and potency to the lifeline.

The line of Mars is more often absent on the palm than it is present.

There is no apparent significance in its absence.

## The Sun Line

The sun line is also known as the line of Apollo or line of success. In Chinese elemental symbolism it is called the minor Fire line.

The start of this line is variable depending on its length, but it always rises vertically toward the third or ring finger and terminates immediately below this finger. The line is often absent, but when it does appear, it adds an inner depth and a more personal quality to creative expression. It can be seen as channeling energies toward the third finger, supplementing the expression of this finger. Therefore, when the line is present, the third finger should be examined to see how capable the person is at expressing the qualities provided by the sun line. If the finger is thick, then the qualities are expressed more directly; if thin, less so. If short, the qualities are expressed quite powerfully, and if long, with more subtlety.

Subtlety, diplomacy, and tact are qualities found in people with this line. They have an awareness of their environment and an ability to mediate and influence people and situations to their advantage or creatively. The longer the line and the closer the line starts to the bottom of the palm, the more inner and personal expression is channeled outwardly and is used creatively to succeed in life. The line also brings about a certain amount of determination in achieving or creating. In general people with this line find creative expression easier and are good at it. They don't have to try so hard to express themselves fully and find personal fulfillment.

Short, lightly drawn, striated, or broken sun lines all show a lacking in power and expression of this line and its qualities.

## An Intuitive Look at the Sun Line

This line or lines are sometimes thought to be lines of success. This is partly true, but they are also connected with an ability some people have to sense or work with what we might feel is an unseen or mysterious element in human life.

For instance, someone phoned me yesterday and asked if she could come and see me. It was someone I had not met before and knew nothing about, but she had been talking to a mutual friend, so she knew about me. In this conversation, or conversations, things had happened that were outside my awareness. The events were in the darkness, so to speak, outside my light. In that darkness all manner of things are happening all the time, things that are connected with our personal lives but of which we have no awareness. Occasionally, though, they come into our personal spheres of awareness. These events outside our personal experiences can come into our lives, enriching or taking away, producing opportunity or misfortune. The sun line depicts people who link strongly with those hidden processes. Perhaps they cannot explain this consciously, but they know how to use them, how to make them work for them, so their lives are enriched by those hidden events.

It is in this way the lines can represent success in that what is hidden is bent toward their service, toward fulfilling their lives, toward supplying their needs.

## The Mercury or Hepatica Line

The line of Mercury is also known as the hepatica or the minor Air line. The line starts either at the bottom of the mount of Lunar or close to and even touching the lifeline. The line runs up the palm toward the little finger or the finger of Mercury and usually terminates just below it, giving the line its name.

There has always been a lot of confusion about this line and its meaning. I feel that it represents the need to communicate and express a part of the self—a very personal and sometimes hidden part from deep within. Or it may depict an urge or a drive toward having something to say, having something to contribute, which is deeply personal and is almost a giving of the self.

Fundamentally the line is linked with communicating and relating to society and not about giving anything that is material. So people with a well-marked line may find they are attracted to the media or communications of some sort. But their expression may tend to be far more subtle or on a one-to-one or personal basis with others.

The line adds expression to the fourth or little finger, and this finger must be studied to see how capable and fluently it can express these added energies. If the little finger is weak or short and looks as if there were a lacking in the area of communication, then there could be conflict or frustration in having the drive to communicate something of oneself but not having the equipment to do so. The result of this could be tension or stress within the person.

### Breaks or Striations in the Line of Mercury

If the line of Mercury has many breaks or is striated, as is not uncommon, this shows that the channel or line for communication has not been well developed. Therefore these people may lack an understanding of what it is they have to express. They may also lack fluency of communication, creating tension or stress and perhaps a feeling of not being understood by others.

### The Digestive System and the Line of Mercury

It is often said that this line shows problems with the digestive system particularly if it is very broken or has many striations. I feel this can be the result of the underdeveloped channel of expression and communication—a lacking in the abilities or qualities needed to communicate something of one's self where there is a desire to do so.

### Strong Line of Mercury

If the line is very strong and thick, then the desire to communicate is strong and well developed.

### Line of Mercury Starting Within the Mount of Lunar

If this line starts from within the mount of Lunar, then the expression is more intuitive, imaginative, and there is an inner wisdom to be communicated.

### Line of Mercury Starting from the Lifeline

If the line starts from or around the lifeline, then the expression is more practical, conventional and is more likely to be "earthed" in some way. In other words, the expression will take on a more material bias. The person will want some recognition, through either financial reward or public acclaim, to confirm his more practical wisdom.

### An Intuitive Look at the Line of Mercury or Hepatica Line

The line has in it power to flow from what is the stronghold of the ego, the stronghold of the self and the identity, and away toward the head line or heart line or even farther toward the third and fourth fingers. In it is implied the overflowing of the self, of the person's wealth and goodness. The self is communicating, perhaps in thought, perhaps in emotions, or maybe in some act of self-giving.

It indicates people extending themselves beyond their immediate welfare, their immediate survival, their immediate families. The mount of Venus can be thought of as a castle, a mountain or hill upon which the personality dwells and isolates itself from contact with "outsiders." What is beyond that is the domain that isn't the immediate self, as in a way language is or as emotions that extend toward others are. So this line has this sense of flowing out. Its strength or depth suggests how fully the people realize themselves beyond their ego. In a way it is a spiritual line. It shows a development of the self in a social sense, a wider life than mere survival or protection of the ego.

There is also suggestion that the people may be producing something or living in a way that they may leave behind things that will live beyond their immediate lives. So in this sense the line connects with the spiritual life. It indicates the degree or amount people leave themselves behind, in both a physical and personal sense. For example, my mother died recently. I am her only son. The only possessions she left behind I carried away in a small envelope: bits of paper and torn photos, most of which went in the wastepaper bin. Some people leave art treasures, houses, or their own socially remembered words and deeds.

If there is a line, on a woman's hand particularly, that moves from within the lifeline in a similar direction to the line of Mercury (toward the third or fourth fingers), it suggests she has an extraordinary ability to give of herself in love. It is a wondrous line. It is a power only a few people have to make a special sort of stand in life. It is not a weakness or a fear or surrender to someone else. It is a joyous giving of their lives in love to other beings. It is something a few humans have learned to do. It might be

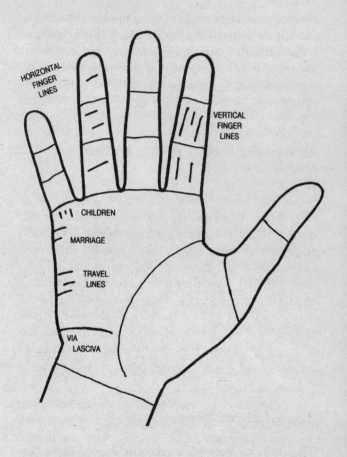

*Secondary Lines*

that the woman gives her life to her family or occasionally to society or other people, but it is often to a man. But this line has the power of the spiritual life in it. It is a breaching of the walls of the ego, that castle, that domain, and a flowing into self-giving.

## An Intuitive Look at the Via Lasciva Line

Some hands have a line that moves from the inner part of the hand on the mount of Lunar to the outer part of the hand toward the thumb. This indicates that if these people have not let their own innermost selves, their own real selves, extend into their external lives, they tend to live lives reflecting or expressive of the past. They develop some part of themselves that links them back to the past. It is as if they lived off their traditions; as if they had not taken up their own personal lives, as if they longed for the world not to change (see pages 216–17).

## The Girdle of Venus

The girdle of Venus is a crescent-shaped line occasionally found on the palm below the fingers and above the heart line. It normally runs from around the area of the first and second fingers across to the area of the third and fourth fingers. This line brings to the person a heightened emotional sensitivity. The person's emotions and sexuality are more quickly stimulated, but this stimulation is emotionally quite shallow and more open to mental control. If this line has many breaks or striations, then it heightens the sensitivity but with more emotional depth if the line is well drawn.

One could say that although people with this line are more easily excited or stimulated, they have a lot less personal and emotional investment involved.

## Other Secondary Lines

There are also smaller lines to look out for when you analyze a hand.

## The Marriage or Relationship Lines

The marriage lines or relationship lines are found on the percussion side of the hand below the little finger. They are horizontal lines just above the beginning of the heart line.

The lines not only represent marriages but also represent major relationships within the person's life—relationships that have been solid enough to leave their mark on the person and the direction of his life. They do not indicate the number of partners the person may have had or his promiscuity. I have seen one clear, well-drawn marriage line on a man who had affairs with many women throughout his life, but he married only once, and he never wished to leave that relationship. The marriage was one to which he was committed, while the affairs made little impact upon his life. In fact, people who have many affairs tend to have only one or two marriage lines. This is because the affairs carry little weight and only the major relationships are marked. People who have several marriage lines— perhaps three, four, or more—tend to have few affairs, but a greater personal investment is made in each relationship. Therefore several major relationships are marked on the hand.

The marriage lines are read from the lower part of the hand nearest the wrist, up toward the little finger. The lower lines represent earlier relationships, and those nearest the fourth or little finger are the most recent.

## Age and the Marriage Lines

The distance between the lines gives a clue to the time between relationships. Experience in reading these lines will allow you to be able to gauge this time distance. It is helpful to ask the person at what age his or her first marriage or major relationship started. This will help in learning to judge the age at which a relationship occurred.

## Strength or Weakness of the Marriage Lines

The longer and more solid the line, the longer the relationship or more significance it has within the person's life. The weaker, thinner, or shorter the line, the less the significance carried and the shorter the relationship.

## One Marriage Line

A person with only one marriage line is likely to want only one major marriage or relationship in life. If there is a split in that relationship, he or she is unlikely to be the one to initiate the break and is prone to be unhappy with change in a relationship.

## Several Marriage Lines

A person with three or four lines is more likely to initiate a break in a marriage or relationship and move on. These people can sometimes look toward new pastures before ending current relationships. They are less likely to be able to make very long-term commitments within their relationships or may even choose relationships that they see as having less commitment.

Some books have noted that as the relationships happen in the person's life, then the lines appear. But I have seen young people with little or no marital experience but with lines marked already, so in my opinion they do suggest the nature of people regarding their relationships. But if one line is marked and that relationship fails, then other lines can appear at a later stage.

## Children or Fertility Lines

Children or fertility lines are marked directly beneath the little finger as vertical lines. These lines usually cross the marriage lines. They show the desire for children and not the exact number of children a person may have.

With contraception today, people can limit how many children they have. Not only do these lines show a desire for children, but they also show an ability to work within a caring profession, helping people as a nurse or doctor or looking after children. They show a caring, parental side to the nature. They indicate the degree to which a person is capable of giving himself in a self-sacrificing way as a parent does with a child. I have often noticed in women who have children that there are the same number of strong and clearly marked lines as children.

These lines are not an indication that the person can have or will have children. They have been noted on women who have never had children but did have the desire and may have found other ways of giving themselves in a nurturing manner.

## The Via Lasciva Line

The Via Lasciva line or the subsidiary Water line runs from the bottom of the mount of Lunar across toward the lifeline, which it sometimes touches or crosses. The line was dramatically described by Cheiro as indicating "unbridled sensuality and passion; and where it cuts through the line of life it indicates death. But a death usually brought about in connection with the licentiousness that it denotes." So it is clear how this line received its name Via Lasciva, "lascivious" meaning "lustful."

We can disregard this interpretation. The line is often absent on the palm. It is present on people who are very sensitive to stimulants and drugs and who can easily become dependent upon them. People with this line are often lacking in drive, power, or influence in the outer physical world. They therefore frequently find a vehicle through which they can live their lives to provide input and stimulus. The vehicle might be drugs, physical stimulation, or even another person's life, fulfilling desires or needs they cannot fulfill themselves.

This line is not as wildly exciting as it sounds. For example, it may be found on people who find it difficult to effect changes in their lives and who constantly look for external power and intervention to help. The stronger and longer this line, the more these qualities are indicated, particularly when the line touches or crosses the lifeline. The lighter and weaker the line, the lesser the qualities.

## Vertical Finger Lines

The vertical lines found on the fingers show an excess of energy flowing through the fingers. It shows that the person is drawing on his or her energies and possible exhaustion or tiredness.

## Horizontal Finger Lines

The horizontal lines found on the fingers show the barring and obstruction of the flow of energies through the fingers.

## The Travel Lines

The horizontal lines sometimes found on the mount of Lunar, often called travel lines, show a subconscious stress or restlessness, a dissatisfaction, that may lead people to change the circumstances in their lives or to travel.

# 13

## Taking Handprints

### To Make a Print of a Person's Hand

To make a good quality print of a palm, the following materials are required, all of which are available from an art shop:

- A square piece of linoleum board
- A roller
- A tube of watercolor paint (preferably black)

Squeeze some watercolor paint onto the linoleum board. After some practice at taking prints in this way you will be able to judge how much is the right amount. Try a length just under a quarter inch to start with, and adjust from there.

Take the roller, and roll the paint evenly over the board. The aim is to get a fairly even layer of paint across the roller. Then, using the roller, roll the paint onto the person's palm, starting from the fingers and moving down toward the lower part of the palm. You may have to roll several times to cover the whole hand. Make sure you cover areas such as the bottom of the fingers, the side of the hand, and the middle area of the palm. Do not apply great pressure on the roller to reach these areas; if you do, the paint will go into the creases on the hand and the lines on the print will not be very clear. Instead try to maneuver the roller into the hand to cover all areas of the palm. The aim is to cover the hand with a thin layer of paint without filling in all the lines. You will probably have to experiment a few times at first to get the right amount.

Once the palm is covered with paint, place the hand onto a plain sheet of paper. When the hand is placed on the paper to make a print, make sure the forearm is level with the flattened hand. This ensures that more of the palm surface will be in contact with the paper. Ask the person to place the hand on the paper in a natural position, without stretching or tensing the hand.

Apply firm but gentle pressure on the hand to make sure no distortion in the print occurs. Take a pencil, and lightly trace around the outline of the hand (a very thin pencil or pencil lead will work best). Lift the hand (the paint should make the paper stick to the palm), turn the palm up, and using your fingers, gently apply pressure to the middle of the palm and the base of the fingers to make sure that those areas of the palm that are often not in contact with the paper are printed properly. The paper can now be removed from the palm.

Now take a separate print of the thumb. Repeat

the tracing procedure with the thumb pad gently pressed against the paper. It may take a number of attempts to produce a clear print, but only trial and error will develop your skill in this procedure. If after two or three attempts you fail to get a clear print, you may find it necessary to wash the palm and reapply the paint to prevent smudging on your subsequent attempts to get a clear print. Because the paint is water-based, you should have no difficulty in washing it away.

Once you have made a successful print of each hand, it is useful to note some personal details about the person, for example, date of birth, left- or right-handed, profession, marital status or sexual preference, number of children, and so on. Virtually any biographical information can be useful in reading palms. Particular characteristics and peculiarities of a person should be included in the profile. You may also wish to include such physical characteristics as the skin quality, color, and so on that cannot be captured by the print. Remember to make a note of the date that the print was taken since it will serve as a point of comparison for other prints made at a later date.

With your prints dated you will be able to observe the changes in the hands and record the time taken for the change to occur. It is interesting, even exciting, to see for yourself the changes that can occur in a hand. The changes in the palm will show how much change has occurred in the person. Also people often come back and tell you that they have a new line on their hand, and quite often it will be seen from the earlier prints that they had not noticed it before.

# 14

## Hand Analysis

If you are coming to hand analysis for the first time, there is a lot of information to absorb. It is unlikely that you will remember it all when you first attempt a hand analysis, but try to absorb the basics and remember that you cannot read just one line or characteristic in the hand. The whole hand must be taken into account. An understanding of this synthesis of qualities and characteristics will be something that will develop from actually reading hands.

As you read more hands, you can keep referring back to this book to confirm what you have seen and the interpretation. It is easy to remember a mark or quality when you have actually seen it and there has been a positive response from the person in your interpretation. Therefore the book is meant to be reasonably simple and should serve as a good basis for developing your hand analysis further.

Understanding the quadrants in the palm is important. Build your relationship with their meaning so that you understand the flow of the lines across and through them. You need not then remember all the positions of the lines because you will have an understanding of the flow and direction within the quadrants. This is rather like understanding the culture and beliefs of an unfamiliar country that you may be traveling through. With such an understanding, many of the small events and things you see will be understandable.

Hand analysis becomes so much easier if you take time to understand the basic elements in the hand rather than try to remember configurations, such as the forked end of the head line. With the basic understanding of the quadrants and overall aspects of human nature a line is connected with, the differences in the lines are self-explanatory. You will then be reading from an understanding of how the different qualities that are part of a human being interact with one another.

So don't worry too much about remembering. Think more about understanding. Apart from the ability to read the hands there is also an ability to give advice and direction required. The simplest way to do this is to take information from the hand and lines and present it to the person.

## Approaching a Hand Analysis

The first thing to keep in mind when reading some-one's hands is that you need not say any more than you are personally capable of picking up or interpreting from the hands you are studying.

It is easy to fall into the trap of feeling under pressure to say a great deal about the person, and at times, particularly for the inexperienced reader, you can easily run out of things to say. At that point you may find yourself bolstering the reading with comments you feel are not strictly true or else mumbling on over the same areas or overemphasizing the points that you have already made. At the end of the day you can only offer what you have to give, and this is a good habit to start with. The reading always has more communicative power if you are comfortable and clear about what you are saying.

Another mistake is to rush the reading and start talking before you are ready and before you have properly studied the hand. This is another pressure that is often felt during what seems like a long silence when you are taking in everything from the hands. You need not be silent during this study time. I often talk to people about the subject of hands, giving them bits of information about hand reading. While I am talking, I am taking a good look at all the areas of their hands.

It is a good idea to tell the person what sort of reading you are going to give. Many people are under the impression you might be fortune-telling. I often describe what I am giving as a physical, mental, and emotional character analysis. I tell them I am not attempting to predict the future but am looking at direction and possible life choices they might make from what I can see of their character and makeup. The information I give will be based on their attitudes and character as it stands at that time.

The more palms you read, the more familiar you will be with what you can offer in the reading. Therefore with experience you will define for yourself just the type of reading you are capable of giving. You will discover what areas you shine in and where your own areas of difficulty or lack of definition are.

Each palmist has a different way of expressing what he or she sees in the hand. Palmists emphasize different aspects of the hand. Some are more spiritual or mystical; others, more practical and down-to-earth. In your own readings you can therefore find your own approach. Because of this, it is helpful to visit several palmists to learn from their approach or presentation.

When you are giving readings, people will come to you seeking particular sorts of information. You will find your own personal interests and talents add a special quality to what you present in your readings to people. It might be a quality to do with work and what is most attractive and successful in that area; it might be in regard to relationships, because you have yourself seen so much difficulty in that area; or it might be in the spiritual quest where your own special insight shines. Whatever it is, recognizing your own special area allows it to flow more fully into your hand analysis, thereby enriching it.

After saying what sort of reading you will give, it is helpful to start describing the person's hands. Say whether the hands are large or small, describe the fingers, nails, and any other qualities, and then move on to the lines on the palm. If the person doesn't know already, show him the major lines, such as the life, head, and heart lines. Briefly describe what each represents. When I do this, I find it gives me time to take a long look at the hands and fully take in what I am seeing before I actually start the interpretation or reading.

When I first started reading hands, I found I would rush into it without a detailed study of the hands. Five minutes after I had completed the reading I would have all sorts of information popping into my head about the hands I had just read. By this time, though, it was too late because I had already finished the reading. This was frustrating because the best things I had realized had not been shared with the person. By taking time to make a complete study of the hands first, you allow yourself to absorb fully and digest information from the hands. As no one characteristic of the hand can be taken on its own, all characteristics must be balanced against the others. Therefore it is important to do this complete study of the hands.

I always make a point of taking hold of the person's hands while I am making the reading. This contact can communicate to you the warmth, tension, dampness of the hands, along with other minor but useful pieces of information.

Try to carry out the reading in a well-lit environment; otherwise you can very easily miss some minor markings and subsidiary lines. It has often been suggested by palmists that you must read hands only after taking prints and studying them carefully. Only then should your conclusions be made. I must admit that I very rarely read a palm from a print, and I don't really enjoy sitting down and studying the prints on my own. I enjoy the contact and interaction with people, and I find there is so much more information to be picked up by sharing your conclusions and questions with them.

To find your own place within hand analysis, develop your own way of going about it. I see a hand reading as a two-way communication. I don't see the purpose of the hide-and-seek type of reading that a lot of people expect, where the people being analyzed keep very quiet and expect you to tell them all manner of detailed information about their past and future, and when you ask a question, they become very evasive and look at you as if you have just broken the rules.

A good and constructive reading in my view would proceed in the following way:

- First, look at the hands. Make an interpretation about the character and major events in the person's life. This may lead on to some questions on particular points that need clarification.
- Second, you need to ask the person his opinion of what has just been said and if he has any questions. I usually ask people what they really want in life, where they see themselves going, what their problems have been.

You can ask any other questions you may feel like asking. In fact, don't be afraid to ask questions. People can refuse to answer if they so wish, and it is really the only way to learn and verify what you have seen in the hand. It is important you do this to check your accuracy. But more important, when you get information from people, you can weigh it up with what you have interpreted from their hands and be able to give some really constructive and helpful advice. For example, you could point out other ways of achieving their aims; explain weaknesses to be aware of, clarify their potentials and leanings. The list is endless.

What is important is that by interacting with the people, you can find out what is most significant to them at this time and what advice they are really looking for. If you don't do this, you may well unknowingly miss the area they are really seeking information about. A doctor does not look at the body and diagnose what the problem is without the patient's saying a word. He has to ask questions. He has to help the patient guide him to the right diagnosis by two-way communication, and this is not unlike reading hands.

With more experience you may find that your questions are fewer and more direct and the "diagnosis" is found quicker.

- Remember to check if the subject is left- or right-handed. Look for the differences between left and right hands; it is these differences that show you the balance between inner and outer life, potential and actual, family influences and individuality. When you look for differences between the hands, don't just look at the lines, but look at the fingers, thumbs, nails, and all the characteristics of the hand. At times you will find a remarkable difference between left and right hands.
- When reading hands, always ask the person's age. From this you can judge events that have

passed and those that are quite current in the hands. I often get the comment "You should know that already," but I don't know of any method to tell a person's age apart from guessing like everybody else.

- It is a good idea to get a routine in the way you do the interpretation. This helps you to cover all areas of the hand without missing something. For example, start with early life, the point of independence, and major events in life up-to-date. Go on to intellectual and then emotional qualities, relationships, and children. Next look at the person's direction in life and what he is creating of his future.

- This is obviously a very rough guide and must be flexible to cope with the many different hands that you will encounter, but nevertheless this routine gives you some pointers in taking the reading.

- It is good to end with a summary of what you have actually said and what you feel are the most important points. From there you can get into asking and taking questions to build further on what you have already said. I find if it is done correctly and a good rapport has been established that this last part is the most rewarding for both sides.

- When you are reading hands, there is often a nagging feeling in the back of your mind, or a perception or intuition you are aware of, or something that seems very obvious. If you are not careful, these pieces of information can be overlooked and disregarded. This intuitive information or hunches can frequently be very accurate, though, and need to be shared with the person. The more you are aware of this information, the more you will encourage it to come out. There is no need to put such information out as a bold bald statement. It can be broached as a question or suggestion.

- You must try to use the knowledge that you have gained in reading hands together with your inner intuitive wisdom and to balance the two as well as try to improve and explore both these areas. Sometimes you must go out on a limb and express a feeling that you have. You may be wrong, but that is all part of the learning process. But don't be surprised when the response that comes back shows you are right. There is great personal satisfaction gained from developing your knowledge and intuition. Try always to push yourself a bit further rather than stay overcautious

- Keep in mind that you may often be put in a position of power and respect by the person and that people may well act on or react to the information or advice that you are giving. So be thoughtful about what you say. Of course you can be critical, but at the same time try to be constructive. It's no good being critical if you offer no advice or alternative. It's no good making sweeping statements without explaining why you have said what you did and what the implications are. The whole point of doing a reading is to offer helpful advice and insight, and therefore the reading should be upbeat and constructive. Don't offer dead ends with your reading, but instead give people long, stretching roads.

## Judging Timing in the Lines

Timing is probably the most difficult technique in hand analysis to master and will only really be learned after a good deal of practice and experience. This is because hands come in all different shapes, sizes, and proportions, and you can't really put a measure to a line on a hand and find an exact date or time. Hands are as individual as the different natures of people, and so a judgment must be made on every hand that you look at. Nevertheless experience has shown that it is a very useful skill and can help define particular experiences in people's lives. When you have learned the art of putting a date to a difficult time in the person's life, it can give him and yourself a testing point to work from in the reading.

There are many different systems of timing explained in various books, and some are very complex and seemingly very accurate. I have found that real accuracy has only been achieved after a great deal of experience and never by exact measurement. The art of judging time in a hand can, however, be surprisingly correct. So this aspect of hand analysis relies more heavily on developing intuition than complicated formulas.

An approach that I find works well is to apply a very simple scale to the lines and to work from that in developing the personal skill and judgment (see

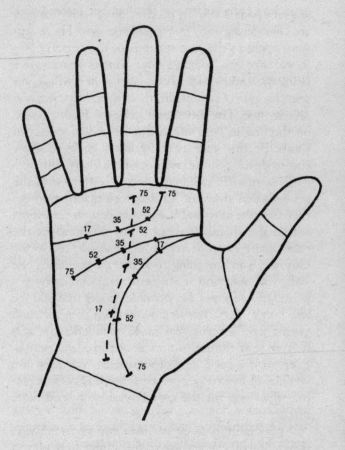

*Timing Scales*

diagram page 233). To do this, divide any line you are considering into four equal sections. These sections apply to the four quarters of the person's life. If we take the average life span as seventy-five years, the end of each section of the line will represent the ages of seventeen, thirty-five, fifty-two, and seventy-five. The years tend to be more compressed on the line in later life and more widely spaced in youth. So this scale is really just a guide to allow you to develop more accuracy from there on.

To start with, you may need to confirm with the person when an event actually took place, and from there on you may find it easier to date other events within that hand. If there is any doubt about the time of any event, don't be afraid to ask; this is the only way you are going to learn. As you learn the skill, you may find it easier to date events over a period of five years, for example, to say that you see an event that happened between twenty and twenty-five. As you feel more confident, you can narrow your timing to a two- or three-year period. Even with a good deal of experience you may find you are off by one or two years, but it is very satisfying when you hit the correct year more and more often.

I personally date events over two or three years depending on the accuracy I feel I have in reading a particular palm. When you have the exact date of one event in a palm, then it becomes easier to time other events on the same palm. After gaining experience in timing, you will find you have forgotten the scale altogether and that you are relying solely on your own judgment.

## Past and Future in Timing

You must keep in mind when you are looking at a hand that you are also looking at a living being, an animal. Our bodies do not keep notes of the months and years in the same way as our rational minds do. There is no calendar in our hands, so we must not expect to see events neatly marked on the hands. But we are marked by experience. Pain and joy do etch their marks into our bodies. We see it in the faces and postures of those around us. We see it also in the hands.

Therefore we are looking at people as they are at this moment. There is no past and no future, just the state in which they are *now*. Even when we see past events marked on the palm, we see them only because they are a part of the person at this moment. The past event has shaped the person in some way and is a living part of the present being.

When we look at future directions, they can only be suggested by understanding the present state of the person. Everything that is marked in the hand represents the present, who the person is at this moment and what he will create of possible coming events out of his present attitudes and gathered experiences.

Timing is a very important part of making a reading because it allows you entry into a person's life. Through it you can identify events that he can recognize and confirm. This helps in gaining the person's confidence in your competence. Once you have gained that confidence, it becomes much easier to work with him to find out what the person is actually looking for in the reading.

Timing acts like an anchor in a reading and really brings the reading into the physical world, relating it to things that are very personal to the person. Without this, a reading can be full of qualities and characteristics that are not connected to or integrated into the actual life of the person.

Looking at the events in people's lives gives you an idea of the things that have shaped their lives and how they have coped with them. When events are seen to be marked in the future, you must not fall into the trap of predicting events or fortune-telling. Instead help the people understand that all future trends, events, and disturbances are a product of their present states of being. Therefore such events can be altered; they are just projections of who the people are right now. In this way you can give the direction in which you see them moving, explaining it as one of many possible directions. They are going in that direction because of who they are at the moment, not because of fate or destiny.

It is true that generally people must initiate change in their characters and attitudes, and quite often people do follow similar patterns throughout their lives. So predicting future directions may well turn out to be correct. But I make a point of saying, "This looks like the direction you are going in, and the chances are that you will continue on that course. But it is by no means set. It is up to you to alter or change it." This approach helps them become more aware of the route they are taking and therefore alter course if they feel it necessary.

## Timing and the Fate Line

When applying timing to the fate line, you must remember this line is often not fully drawn. In other words, its start may appear well up the palm. Therefore you must apply your judgment about timing to how far up the hand the line begins and terminates. If it starts very low on the hand, then the qualities of the line are effective at a very early age, if it starts in the middle of the palm, then middle age is suggested, and so on to the termination of the line

If the fate line starts halfway up the hand, do not quarter the line, but consider it as beginning at the base of the palm for your measurements. The scale must be applied to the hand rather than the line itself, and you will need to judge from the beginning and ending of the line the ages that are implied. It may be useful to divide the length of the palm into quarters to give you some kind of scale to start with until you are able to judge for yourself.

## Timing in the Lines of Marriage and Relationships

As you look at the lines of marriage or relationships, it again comes down to experienced judgment. The lines that are marked lower on the hand represent relationships from earlier in life, and lines that are marked higher are relationships later in life. The greater the distance between the lines, the greater the number of years between the relationships. You might ask at what age any particular relationships occurred, and matching this information to the lines that you see on the hand will help you learn to judge the timing of the major relationships in a person's life.

## Fingernail Flecks as Means of Timing

I find the white flecks on the nails extremely accurate as indicators of any disturbances over the last six months (see pages 113–14 for more details).

## Other Signs of Events and Changes

Events are most commonly marked as bar lines or subsidiary lines crossing the major lines, interrupting the energy flow. As previously explained, other signs of disturbances can be islands, stars, and dots. Positive signs may show as breaks in lines, which indicate great change, and as branches, which show expansion.

Lack of definition, chaining, and striations in lines show periods of weakness and low energy. All these events are most commonly marked on the lifeline and often reflected on other lines involved.

Remember, events marked on the lifeline show effect on the person's outer physical life, on the heart line they indicate influences on the emotional life, on the head line they show an influence on the reasoning and mental perception, and on the fate line they depict influence on the direction and drive in life.

When looking for events in the palm, you are looking for the change in the energy flow of the line—an alteration, interruption, or redirection. When these are identified, you can then try to put them into a time frame. It would be impossible to make a list of the exact causes of all these different markings. Life is so varied and there are so many possibilities, but you will know the qualities and results of these markings and events from the lines themselves. Look at the lines to see how they have affected the balance of the subject and how or whether recovery has been achieved and any positive growth and expansion marked.

It is important to find out the details of the event or situation from the person so you can learn from and study the effects shown within the person. This will also help you to understand how certain events show effects that are both physical and emotional or physical and mental, enabling you to relate markings on different lines to the same time and event. When you have an understanding of the cause and effect of past events, you will become clearer in explaining future directions and potentials.

# 15

## Intuitive Hand Analysis

"Intuition" is defined in the *Concise Oxford English Dictionary* as the "immediate apprehension by the mind without reasoning—or immediate insight." Most often we think of intuition as knowing something without having gathered information about it through our senses or through previous thought.

In films and fiction the intuitive person has often been depicted as a mysterious stranger who meets people and can tell them facts about themselves, about their futures and pasts, without any exterior information. The characterization may portray them as having occult or mysterious powers or as employing spirits or demonic forces. Such portrayals show us the common conceptions people have of human abilities like intuition.

The enormous amount of research into how the mind works has shown people rational explanations of intuition. We can use words now such as "unconscious and subliminal perception" instead of "spirits and occult forces." Because of this change in people's perception of this faculty in recent years, many modern films show the intuitive person as being a highly evolved alien from another world, or as someone having developed faculties previously slumbering, or as having used technology to enhance his mind. From this we can see there are a number of ways intuition is explained. They range from communion with the devil, the help of disembodied spirits, clairvoyance and telepathy, latent human faculties, using the unconscious mind and trickery to training the mind to work with its latent faculties.

## How Intuition Works

Recently, while I was driving quite fast around a large traffic circle, a car pulled out in front of me from one of the side roads. The driver gave no signals, so I was uncertain if he was going to carry on across my path or take the next exit off the circle. I immediately pulled across to get behind him. This all happened very quickly, so there was no time to reason at length about what to do. The driver actually took the next turning off, so I could have driven across his path. The safest bet, however, was to follow behind. Afterward, with hindsight, this all could be reasoned out and the decision analyzed. At the time, however, I needed intuition because of the speed at which it all happened. Intuition in this case was the result of unconscious or subliminal experience of driving gathered over many years, called upon and expressed as automatic or intuitive response.

In this case one could say I acted intuitively—that is, without rational thought. *The Oxford Companion to the Mind* claims that in fact we are all using intuition all the time, in that we do not often go through the steps of logically examining an argument before making a decision. "In this sense," the book says, "almost all judgements and behaviour are intuitive." The book goes on to say that "women's intuition" may be largely the result of subtle and almost subliminal cues arising from gestures, snippets of conversation, and gathered knowledge of behavior patterns and motivations in social action.

So from what has already been said, intuition can arise from:

- Gathered experience that has not all been made conscious at the time of the intuitive response. This experience might be a special area of study, such as medicine, motor engineering, or hand analysis, or it might be general, such as the everyday life experience of people and social interactions. This form of intuition can be examined afterward and with time the sources of it be explained or identified.

- Cues given us by other people in their behavior, facial expressions, clothing, speech and speech tones, posture, and movements. Study of intuition arising from these show that each of us in fact gathers an enormous amount of information about others within a few seconds of meeting. Such information usually remains unconscious unless we take time to examine carefully and express what our impressions of the people were and what we have concluded about them. An overall summary of this mass of gathered information can arise as a hunch or an "intuitive" feeling of like or dislike, trust or mistrust. If such feeling responses are explored, however, details may be made conscious about the person being considered.

Although it is not yet proved by research, some thinkers such as Carl Jung and Rupert Sheldrake see individual human consciousness like an island in a huge ocean in which there are countless other islands. Above the surface of the water—waking self-awareness—there is separate existence, with definite boundaries where the shore meets the sea. Beneath the surface, however, one island is connected to all other islands. The land stretches away under the waves and rises here and there into other islands. So, it is thought, personal awareness, beneath our everyday consciousness, shades off into a connection with a collective unconscious we all share. Through this connection we may be able to arrive at insights into other people otherwise denied to us. In this way questions or inquiries about particular people will draw information pertaining to them from the enormous collective unconscious.

## Examples of Intuition

In our lifetimes most of us have personal experiences of at least one of these forms of intuition. The following account is an example of the second form of intuition—cues given us by others.

While teaching in Japan, I was staying for a few days with a family in which the wife was Japanese and the husband American. I was asked to act as counselor to the wife, Hiroko, who was experiencing psychosomatic pain in the chest and general anxiety. The way I work is to have people allow their bodies and voices free expression so innate tensions can be released. Hiroko quickly began to cough and choke and express signs of emotional and physical struggle, but without being able to say what emotions the choking was connected to. I felt rather lost as I had not known her for long and she gave no other information. So I used my intuitive faculty, asking for help.

Immediately a powerful series of images and feelings arose. They outlined a cultural and personal conflict regarding relationship. Hiroko was pregnant, and my intuition suggested she was terrified that once she had given birth, her husband would find another woman. I said to her, "Is this about Andrew and the baby?" She immediately cried out, "Don't leave me! Don't leave me!" Tears and sobbing about being left followed.

Amazed at this very direct insight into what

was troubling Hiroko, I later wondered how my unconscious had known this, because consciously I had not suspected the fear she expressed. I asked my unconscious where it had got this information. Straightaway a memory arose of an event two days prior to the counseling session. I had been teaching Hiroko how to make bread. During this I had remarked that I thought her baby would be beautiful as it would be a mixture of East and West. Her reply in a slightly subdued voice was "I suppose so." My unconscious had put this together with other bits of information picked up regarding the culture and couple and extrapolated its intuition of her conflict.

The intuitive insight described above shows clearly not only how our unconscious absorbs the minutiae of daily experience but also how it examines these in connection with the other bits of information gathered and extracts possible meaning from them. If we used such a faculty often, we would make conscious a mass of realizations that otherwise might not easily break through the threshold between unconscious and conscious.

In connection with hand analysis here is an example of how this can work. It was experienced by one of the authors.

I had been talking at a dinner table to some of the people around me about hand analysis. Some of them had asked me to look at their hands. In quite a lighthearted manner I had done so. Afterward a woman I had not made any real connection with previously came to me and asked if I would look at her hands and tell her what I could see. As we were both in a hurry at that point, I said I would try to do so within the next few days.

It was about two days later when I sat down with her and told her what I could by examining the lines on her hands. This seemed rather dry, so I said if she didn't mind I would see what I could get from an intuitive reading. She agreed, and I closed my eyes and decided to try to use the image approach. From this two strong pictures arose, describing two different situations. In the first the woman was shown being forced to change her life because an event had pushed her into the change. I described this to her as a big change that had occurred in her life, but it was not at all what she had wanted. I felt she was now living the results of this event and still trying to find her own place in it.

The second picture showed her in a quiet, receptive situation, reading, but with an invisible presence trying to support her with its love. I described this to her as a man who cared for her but had died and was now, according to the impression, trying to support her and make his love known to her.

The woman identified with the first statement immediately. Her husband, after a marriage of many years, left her to live with another woman. This had forced unwanted changes into her life that were still influencing her. We talked this over for a while. Then I asked her what place, if any, did the pictured dead person have in her

life. She immediately started sobbing and told
me that after her husband left her, a good friend
of his became her lover. This man had made her
feel wanted and cared for in a way she had not
known before. He never left his wife, and their
relationship remained a secret. He had died six
weeks ago, and she was mourning his death. So
the image telling of his support brought a lot of
emotion and meant a great deal to her.

This is not a perfect example of intuition because it
was not detailed enough to be undeniably a direct
perception of the woman's life experience, without
previously knowing her history. Even so, it is still a
good example of how intuition can be used in hand
analysis and counseling people. Because the woman
was met at a place frequented by many single
women, some of what was said could have been inferred or extrapolated. Even so, this does not di-
minish the value of intuition. It can focus attention
and draw conclusions from scattered impressions
and unconscious information.

## Intuition as the Highest Probability

One of the factors I have noticed in watching people use their intuitive faculties is how the mind
functions when we ask ourselves a question. One
day my daughter came to me from another room in
our house with her hands behind her back. Play-
fully she asked me what she was holding. At that
moment I was for some reason in a mode of deep

self-perception and could observe some of what was taking place at lightning speed in my mind. A mental scan was occurring that presented likely objects. There was also a filter acting to weed out objects that did not meet a whole list of criteria, such as: What was in the other rooms and not this? What might my daughter temperamentally choose? What topics of conversation had preceded the event? What did her action tell me, and so on?

This all happened very fast, and it is difficult to particularize, but it was obvious that what the computing function of my mind was doing was looking for the highest probability within its points of reference and filtering. What I said within seconds was "banana" because this is what I arrived at as the highest probability. My daughter was amazed and asked me how I did it. It had appeared magical, yet it was based on basic mental functioning and being able to let the mind scan freely and then critically appraise its scan results—i.e., filter out the negative hits.

If we learn to appreciate and use some of these mental processes, we can begin to "think" in a radically new way. It is important to realize that if we start to use these dormant faculties, we will almost certainly start by approaching them with traditional values, unless we have carefully reevaluated the subject. The characterizations in drama mentioned at the beginning of this chapter are examples of these general conceptions of intuition. If we were asked to find the hidden secrets of a person's character without conversing with him or using detective work, we might well revert to using a Ouija board in a spiritualistic séance.

These factors of traditional values may lead many people who use an intuitive faculty to do so in a sort of mental vacuum or hermetically sealed belief system. Because the mind works better when we relax, such belief systems may be useful in giving the person confidence. But such systems often have enormous limitations, in that one would have to remain within the belief system for the faculty to work. If the subject of intuition is understood in a general sense outside such belief systems, however, I believe such understanding can help the faculty of intuition to flower.

## The High Art of Intuition

The highest form of intuitive response to another person is the one described above as accessing the collective unconscious. When this occurs, it does not have the signs of extrapolation or unconsciously taking in the cues from people through their gestures, clothes, voices, and so on. It jumps beyond what information we have received personally and presents a direct perception of things beyond our knowing. This is comparatively rare. It might be compared with the sorts of connections we make daily on the telephone. Usually they are local or individual calls. Only certain people have massive computer and telephone connections worldwide to access information beyond their personal or work domains. When this occurs, information about almost anybody might be accessed. This is like accessing the collective unconscious. In fact, the massive growth of communication technology is giving us a material example of what can apparently take place naturally in the mind.

## Learning Intuitive Hand Analysis

There are several ways of using the intuitive ability we each have. Your own most effective approach will no doubt depend upon your character. If you are a person who looks at life mostly through your feelings, then using these would be quicker than using the imagery or scanning approach. If you use your intellect most of the time, the scanning technique might be best. Or if you are imaginative and use imagery a great deal, this approach would suit you.

To flex and develop your ability, however, there are several techniques you need to practice. These should be used frequently until you feel at ease using them and gain a reasonably clear response each time. At the very start use them in an experimental way. They often work best when you are talking to another person, so you need a friend or friends to practice with. Tell them you are learning the technique and want to see if it will work with them. They can even try it with you and tell you their impressions.

### The Spontaneous Voice Approach

The experience below illustrates one of the approaches to intuition.

A middle-aged Gypsy woman rang my door-bell one day selling heather. She immediately began to tell me things about myself that it seemed to me it was unlikely she knew from other people. She told me I had started a couple of businesses that had not been successful; a close member of family had just had an injury; my son had recently gone into a uniformed service, and I was worried about him. It was correct about the businesses, but that information was not impressive. My brother-in-law had just had a nail go right through his foot at work. My son had just joined the RAF, and her words brought tears to my eyes, much to my surprise.

As she told me these things, before each statement she said, "Now I am going to tell you something true." These words were said ritualistically, almost like a prayer, then she would say things that I had the impression she had not thought about. I was not able to question her about this as it was not easy to have conversation with her. She gave me the Gypsy's curse because I wouldn't pay her the money she demanded. This amused me, as having an Italian background and having explored the unconscious workings of the mind for many years, I well understood the nature of curses and their attempt to mobilize unconscious fears of things such as illness, worrying events, and accidents.

The technique this episode illustrates can be called spontaneous voice. To use it we must learn to speak without our thoughts constantly editing and criticizing what is being said, or at least we must learn to direct the scanning and editing functions of our minds.

The intuitive impressions we have, the information we have gathered unconsciously from whatever source, do not usually rise into clear, conscious awareness. Thinking about what we do not already know is not possible. We only think with the information that we already have or that is easily available. Creative leaps are a jump beyond what is known. So to access what is intuitively understood but not yet consciously recognized, we must use something different from conscious thought.

Focusing on another person and allowing ourselves to speak without forethought are a way of doing this. The unconscious functions that support the action of speech are already well established in fast-searching for memories and information connected with whatever is being spoken about. Associated ideas, feelings, memories, along with the words to express them, all are quickly accessed in the process of speech. The difference is that instead of presenting the process of speech with an outline of what needs to be said, you present it with a blank sheet with only the name of the person at the top.

In reality it is a lot more formulated than that. Here are the steps helpful in using this approach.

1. Hold in mind clearly what you are about to do. This is most important for the first dozen or so times you do it; after that you can simply remember the previous times the function was used. In other words, decide to stop your conscious attempts to find information or use

ready-made answers to the question you are going to ask. Imagine your body, mind, and feelings like keys on a piano, poised ready to respond, but not to your conscious efforts. Hold the picture of yourself standing aside— the part of you that has learned to be concerned about what comes out of your mouth, whether it makes sense, what people are going to think about it, and so on—and let your sleeping dream self respond.

2. Make the decision that you are going to use your voice as a way of expressing what you already intuitively know. The first times you practice this it will be best to do so by yourself or with a friend you are completely relaxed with and who knows you are trying to develop your intuitive ability.

3. Now hold in mind that you are asking for helpful information about the person you are considering. It is of great value if the person —perhaps the friend you are practicing with —actually asks you to tell them what your impressions of her or him are. As you ask for information, remember to see the information you seek as existing unconsciously within yourself. In this way you clarify the need to hold your conscious mind in an open, receptive condition.

4. You can develop the receptive condition of your mind and feelings by taking on a feeling of patient listening or waiting. If you have enjoyed a massage at some time, it is rather like the feeling of letting someone else make the effort while you relax. That is just what you

need to do. Don't struggle. Relax and let your voice be moved from within.

5. The next step is to begin to doodle with your voice. For the very first practice sessions it will help if you sit in the receptive condition, perhaps with your eyes closed, and gently make a humming sound. Take hold of the other person's hand, and in the back of your mind hold the realization you are waiting for information about this person. As you do so, let the humming sound move wherever your voice wants to take it. Let your voice doodle, rather as your hand might with a pencil while you were thinking about something else.

6. To start with, you might find you have an urge to make mumbling, struggling sounds as your voice is getting used to being moved by a level of your mind other than conscious thought or emotion. This is normal and will gradually go as your voice responds more readily and capably to your unconscious intuitions. Eventually you will be able to use this technique without the person in front of you knowing you were not speaking from conscious thought.

7. The step from "normal" speaking to speaking from the intuitive awareness may at first seem a big one. You are only overcoming habit and ideas of what you can and can't do though. The way to gain this remarkably useful tool is to practice, and then practice, and practice again, just as you did when you learned to speak in the first place—practice and play at it.

## The Gypsy Secret

What the Gypsy woman did that is worth understanding was to use a short ritual to jump-start her
spontaneous speaking. Through practice she had
learned that every time she said the words "Now I
will tell you something true," she called on her intuition to produce a result relevant to the person
she was confronting.

Such a ritual need not be made obvious, but if it
is, it makes it more powerful because it puts you on
the spot. Crisis is one of the best stimulants to wake
the powers of the unconscious into expression. The
fact that people know you are going to address
them from something other than a "normal" state
of mind will make them give you their full attention. Their attention helps to pull a powerful response from you.

## The Intuitive Imagery Approach

All the ways we might call on intuition are based
on the way we call on our memories and experiences to respond to everyday life. When someone
asks us what our names or telephone numbers are,
we do not have to struggle to find the answers. The
question itself provokes the response. We witness
the response and tell it to the questioner. It is precisely the same action when we use intuition—except we may need to look in a slightly different
direction within ourselves for where or how the response appears.

If you give a little consideration to how memory responses occur, you will realize that they might come in various ways. Many of our most frequently used memories, such as our names, addresses, or telephone numbers, have long been coded into words. Some things we store as images and express in words only when describing. Or our memories may be stored as emotions or feeling tones.

Usually we allow our inner responses to the demands we make occur with hardly any awareness. We barely notice what happens when we use our resources of skill or memory. In developing access to our intuition, however, we may at first need to use our faculties a bit more consciously. If we do not do this, our old habit of simply accessing memory and the already known information will probably assert itself instead of the intuition. Habits are very powerful, and until we get our intuition well grounded, we need to direct the process consciously. This is not a great task, however.

The imagery approach asks the unconscious to present information about the person in the form of a picture, a symbol, or a moving tableau. This is easy for the unconscious. It naturally forms imagery around inner material that has not been put into words or been formally thought about. It does this every time we dream. Since the unconscious is a master of this technique, we do not need to develop this aspect of it. What we do need to learn is how to observe the imagery produced when we use the technique.

The steps to learning and using this technique are as follows:

1. First it is necessary to turn your attention away from usual external impressions or trains of thought and clear a quiet, empty space within yourself. This is like having a busy telephone line on which you are always telephoning friends, so there is no space for an incoming call. An easy way to do this is to learn how to watch the screen of your awareness and observe what is happening on it.

To learn this, sit comfortably alone or preferably with a friend you can practice with. Close your eyes, and notice what you are feeling in your body, whether it is comfortable, tense, warm, cold, etc. Whatever you notice, report it to your partner or speak it quietly to yourself. Do not develop a conversation with your partner; simply report your observations in a few words.

Go on to observe what is happening with your feelings. Notice whether you feel sad, calm, irritated, jubilant, etc. This might be a new thing for you, but see if you can put into words what you observe.

Notice next what thoughts and mental images float into consciousness. Catch these fleeting impressions by speaking them to yourself or your friend. Continue with an overall view of what is happening within you for about ten to fifteen minutes. In other words, notice physical, emotional, and mental experience and report it.

This first step needs to be practiced enough times to make you feel easy with it. It is so important you could use it for months and still gain from it. At times you might find emotions arising strongly. Do not be afraid of this. Observe and allow them to be felt. They will gradually fade away, perhaps having led to personal insights. Unless your emotions are free enough to be felt in this way, they are not available to be used as senses in responding to other people.

2. To take self-observation and description into intuitive appreciation of another person, you set the process going in a slightly different way. As you relax prior to self-observation, mentally say to yourself, "I now want my unconscious to present in picture form any intuitions it has of the person before me (or I am asking about)."

3. After this close your eyes and self-observe just as you have done in the previous exercise. Hold the idea that you are particularly looking for mental images. Accept that your unconscious will immediately present a mental picture relating to what you have asked. If you are relaxed and not throwing up masses of self-doubts or conscious attempts to think of answers to your question, a picture will emerge.

Take whatever emerges as relevant to the person you are inquiring about. The picture may not be like a painting in which all the characters are still. It may come as moving scenes. For some people it comes with accompanying emotions and subtle feelings as part of the information.

4. Observe until you feel you have got a sense of

the scene. This may mean that you see the picture but you have no idea of what it means. You may be able to ask your unconscious to help you understand what it represents, and this can bring clarity. If this does not occur, report what you have seen to the person concerned and ask if what is described means anything to him or her. If so, ask him or her to explain. If he or she wants to know more, you can then ask for further images to explore that direction more.

The unconscious can be questioned just as a friend can. Remember that the original response was from a question: What is intuited regarding this person? So to explore more deeply whatever the person's issue is presents no problem. In fact, it is always helpful to ask the person if he has further questions about what has been said.

5. When you first start, practice this with people you feel at ease with. When you have gained confidence and experience, you will feel ready to meet and express your intuitions to strangers.

## The Intuitive Feeling Approach

Using the sensitivity of your feelings instead of images or speech is only a difference of approach rather than technique. Most of what has been said above about the image and speech methods is valid. The practice of self-observation is also necessary before using the feelings for intuition. Then instead of asking for images to explain what is intuited, you ask for shifts in your own inner feelings to explain your intuitions.

The reason for explaining these different paths to the same goal is the basic differences between people. Some people already unconsciously watch their feeling reactions in relationships. They already have expertise and perhaps only need to channel it. Others are more used to imagining situations, playing them through in their minds rather like a drama. Others function through words very fluently. No matter how you see yourself, however, whether verbal, visual, or feeling, do not be put off trying the other approaches. Occasionally switching from one technique to another with the same person can provide different results if you get stuck.

## Counseling People Through Intuition

In actually using intuition with a person who seeks your advice, there are things to apply just as in any other practice or skill. One of the first things to remember is that you are often dealing with very intimate and personal aspects of the person's life. Therefore, if you are going to develop this skill to the point where people will want to seek you out, you must learn the first principle of counseling: confidentiality. What you reveal to yourself and the person before you is to remain confidential and not spoken about to others.

Never speak as if you were seeing the future as it will be. Make sure what is said is spoken of as possibilities arising out of the people's current attitudes and choices. This keeps their minds free of depression arising from feeling trapped in an unavoidable future.

Realize that what you are seeing most likely represents the situation the people are in at the moment and how they feel about it. I once visited a very intuitive woman who told me events that had happened in my life and many things about myself. She went on to say that from what she could see, everything I tried in the future would lead nowhere. There appeared to be no success in relationships, and every avenue in work and endeavor also seemed to be a dead end.

What she failed to tell me, and had perhaps not understood about her own gift, was that the picture she painted was of my mood and fears at the time. I had recently been through divorce, felt terribly torn about what had happened, and from my pain saw all my future as gray and a continuance of my present despair. Her failure to point this out to me, to help me see how my dejection was creating a view of life that stopped me from moving forward confidently was a black mark on her otherwise great skill. I felt terrible for a day after her words, then realized for myself that she was merely reflecting my mood at that time and went forward to create my own future. If you can remain aware of this, you can be of great help to people, who constantly need reminding how their inner moods are creative powers for ill or good.

If you are going to use this ability often, learn some basic counseling skills. If you cannot meet human emotions or pain without trying to repress them or make them better by trite advice, do not set yourself up as someone who can counsel others using the hand. Tell people openly that you are doing it for amusement and nothing more. Counseling skills are not necessarily connected with huge amounts of technical information and diagnosis of other people's conditions. They have mainly to do with learning how to keep quiet, not giving other people advice, and how to help others realize their own problem-solving capacities. One of the greatest of human tendencies is to feel that because we have managed to survive in life to whatever degree we have, we are experts on relationships, in business, in the spiritual secrets of life. That we have learned to use our intuition does not make us great sages or wise in the ways of life. So just present your information and help people find their own decisions.

Another powerful urge in many psychics I have watched, and of course in most of us not skilled in meeting human emotions, is to try to "make things okay" for the person who cries in our presence or shows anger about some life situation. People often need to release emotions, especially if you reveal a side of themselves they have not exposed publicly. In most cases you do not have to "do" anything about this other than be with the person supportingly and sympathetically. If you have not set yourself up as a therapist, you need not get into that role. In fact keep out of it lest you encourage the person to move into a dependent relationship with you.

The person can of course ask questions, and all you need do is to respond from your intuition or from what you can see in the person's hand. Giving information is of great help and need not be pushed into the realms of advice giving or coercion to live in a particular way that is the expression of your own horizons, restraints, fears, and hopes. It is important to clarify for yourself the difference between advice and information.

## Becoming an Accomplished Intuitive

A great deal of healing and problem solving can occur if you can find doorways into a person's hurts, strengths, and difficulties through your intuition. But unfortunately most psychics are awful counselors, and this is why it has been suggested that you learn some level of counseling skill.

As you gain experience, aim to be skilled in what you do. Learn to communicate with your own unconscious; ask questions of it; doubt and explore until you find better performance and clarity. It is important for you to be clear about what you are doing when using your intuition. Recognize honestly that just like any other faculty, such as reasoning, intuition has its limitations. Test your own ability to find out its level of accuracy. Give this a percentage mark if you can so you can look your client in the eye and say something like "I have tried to ascertain the accuracy of my intuitive ability, and I find it is about sixty percent."

The more fully you understand that your unconscious is already an everyday part of your life, constantly providing background information, words in speech, and habitual skills such as walking and writing, the easier you will feel about using its other faculties. Also, understanding how readily it responds to daily requests—for instance, we may not have ridden a bicycle for years, yet we can get on bikes and ride off—helps us to see how we can organize our use of it. Instead of simply asking what you intuitively perceive of people, for instance, you could set up a series of questions so an all-around response could be given to them. You could start with physical health and work through, giving them a very full life reading, covering work, relationships, and spiritual life.

# 16

## Science and Hand Analysis

It was announced as part of national news coverage in the UK during 1993 that a statistical analysis survey had produced unsought-for information that people with whorls in their fingerprints are more prone to high blood pressure and stomach ulcers.

A year or so before, a similar announcement said that an unusual form of research had taken place at a morgue. Deciding to find out once and for all whether there was any connection between the lifeline on the palm and length of life, doctors at the morgue had kept records of the palms of incoming corpses, their ages and lifelines. Their findings showed a definite connection between length of life and the lifeline. Unfortunately I have not been able to gather detailed information about those findings, but more and more frequently modern medicine is confirming what hand analysis has stated for centuries: Your hands may be remarkable indicators of health.

Despite scientific medical opinion treating palm reading as a joke, research at leading universities in recent years has uncovered a great deal of fascinating information about the hands and the markings on them. Such findings have defined what signs on the hands show impending illnesses, genetic abnormalities, and psychological problems. A new field of studies, named dermatoglyphics, states information that is beyond anything traditional hand analysis has been able to define yet is an obvious extension to the ancient curiosity that led to the art, just as chemistry extended and built upon the work of alchemy.

Medicine and hand analysis have a long history. In China the practice of hand analysis was always connected with the health of mind and body. Within Western traditions hand analysis was included in the studies of medical schools as early as the Middle Ages. The Gutenberg printing press in 1475 printed one of Aristotle's books on palmistry. Aristotle was writing on the subject possibly because Hippocrates, the father of modern medicine, had discovered a relationship between the hand and the condition of the lungs.

The development of sophisticated methods of research and physical examination have shown the definite connection between hands and health. Such findings mean that future diagnostic techniques of any depth will certainly contain a thorough examination of the hands, enabling doctors to diagnose everything from alcoholism and schizophrenia to arthritis. In fact, the American Medical Association said in its journal as early as the 1970s, "The human hand is a unique organ from which an extraordinary amount of clinical information may be derived."

## The Womb and the Hand

Life in the womb is the most powerfully formative experience we will ever have physically and perhaps even psychologically. This applies particularly when we are considering the findings of hand analysis.

Levels of prenatal testosterone, circulating in the bloodstream of both male and female fetuses, have been found to influence skin ridge development. These are patterns that last a lifetime unless powerful environmental factors influence them. Robert J. Meier of Indiana University in Bloomington is an authority on the study of human dermatoglyphics. He says that studies done at Harvard over the last decade suggest a connection between the delayed development of the right side of the fetus's brain and excess testosterone circulating in the fetus during the eighth and thirteenth weeks of prenatal development. This can alter an infant's autoimmune system and lead to conditions such as arthritis and asthma. Meier says that the "later the development" of the left side of the brain, "the more ridges are formed [on the hand]. So it's possible that a delay of a week or so could profoundly affect development. It could make quite a difference in the number of ridges formed." Other characteristics, such as left-handedness, are associated with testosterone flow to the left side of the brain. He goes on to say that the palm and fingerprint ridge patterns of alcoholics and people with such mental illnesses as schizophrenia can be seen to be more prominent. Other conditions that show in the palmar ridges are stuttering, Down's and other syndromes, math giftedness, migraines, congenital rubella, and immune deficiencies.

## Palmar Lines and Personal Development

One of the most pronounced and widely acknowledged genetic influences seen on the hand is that found on people with Down's syndrome. The "simian line" nearly always appears on the hands of people with Down's (see pages 159–61). It is a merging of what is usually the heart and head lines of the palm into a single line right across the hand. It also appears on the hands of about 3 percent of the population who do not have Down's syndrome.

This gives us a clue to the importance of the lines, their strength and full development, and how they can indicate physical and mental health. Cathy A. Stevens, M.D., of the University of Utah Medical Center in Salt Lake City, has gathered information that furthers our insight into this. She says: "These things were being talked about in palmistry in the 1800s, and I have some old drawings from India from thousands of years ago indicating certain palmar creases to tell the length of life. I show these to people when I give talks on these creases. It can either be genetic or it can happen from the environment. But something is happening to the baby in utero."

The significance of Cathy Stevens's statement is that one of her case studies is a baby whose mother experienced carbon monoxide poisoning thirteen weeks into her pregnancy. The child had many physical signs of impaired development, such as missing creases where the fingers fold. Stevens also observed that people with Down's syndrome have an extra crease on the upper joint at the tip of the little finger.

Other observed effects of exposure to carbon monoxide during pregnancy are alterations in the main palmar lines. If interference in the development of the fetus through carbon monoxide poisoning causes a lack of full palmar lines and hand development, the opposite can also be taken as true. Therefore a fully developed hand and lines can be taken to show a person who has been able to mature adequately not only in the womb but also outside it in the physical, psychological, and social world he or she has faced.

## Theories of Palmar Line Development

It would seem common sense to believe the creases on the palm are simply lines that have been formed by the folding of the hand. This is in fact one of the theories to explain them. Certain observable facts are not explained by this, however. One of them is the incidence of the simian line on the hands of people with Down's syndrome.

Cathy Stevens's observation of the crease on the little finger of Down's syndrome children where there is no joint to cause a fold suggests lines can be independent of folding. Patients with sickle-cell anemia also show an extra line on the second finger. As the lines develop in the womb, influenced by factors of impairment or support, and change throughout life, there need not be a definite answer to the theories. The important point is they can be seen to be influenced by the successful or impaired development of the individual.

## The Hand and Brain Connectedness

Many acute observations of the world and human experience were made before the scientific approach. Their truth and applicability have been extended by careful scientific testing with today's technology. The system of herbal medicine was developed long before science confirmed the therapeutic value of using herbs. This also applies to such observations as the early banning of pork in the Jewish tradition. Although without the microscope it could not been shown precisely why its consumption could lead to illness, the results of diseases such as trichinosis from uncooked or poorly cooked pork were still there to see.

Similarly many observant hand analysts have said that the shape of the hand, its lines and changes all are connected to the brain and human personality. It is not that the hands are the servants of the brain, but that they have been described as directly influencing each other.

At the University of California, San Francisco, recent studies on monkeys have shown that a finger tapped at regular intervals over a long period causes changes in the brain. The extra stimulus causes the growth of the nerve cell connectors. It has also been found in human fetuses that as the brain develops, its nerve cells grow thousands of axons or projections that enable the hand and fingers to move. So although in the first place it is the brain's growth that enables the hand to grow and function efficiently, stimulus of the hand and fingers then feeds back and produces an expansion of areas of the brain.

## Fingerprints and Left-handedness

In Canada, Stanley Coren of the University of British Columbia, Vancouver, has researched the use of fingerprints as diagnostic tools. He defined eight fingerprint types: a simple arch, sharp arch, left loop, right loop, oval whorl, spiral whorl, round whorl, and double loop. He says of his research, "We found the patterns between left- and right-handers is, in fact, different. What you find is left-handers have simpler patterns. They have more arch patterns and fewer whorls. And we found the biggest difference between the left- and right-handers is on the ring finger." People who are left-handed have more radial loops, which is like an upside-down U. These loops at the center of the fingerprint appear on only about 2 percent of people who are not left-handed. People who are right-handed have these loops, but a person is twice as likely to be left-handed if there are radial loops.

Stanley Coren also observes, "Left-handed people, in truth, get the short end of the stick. Statistically they have reduced life spans and other problems such as allergies, sleep difficulties and slower maturation. The stress of living in a right-handed world may reduce their survival rate. A greater proportion of left-handed people tend to suffer from dyslexia, learning disabilities, schizophrenia and other genetically based abnormalities."

## Fingerprints and Stomach Problems

The first statement in this chapter that whorls in fingerprints suggest an inclination to high blood pressure and stomach ulcers was perhaps forestalled by research at the Johns Hopkins School of Medicine in Baltimore. Marvin Schuster, a professor of medicine and psychiatry at Johns Hopkins, says that patients who have chronic constipation have different fingerprint patterns from people suffering constipation through stress. He says, "About seven to thirteen percent of the general population have arched patterns, and in our group of patients it was seen in fifty-four percent. We felt this would be a genetic marker for these patients."

## Practical Health Signs

Most of the above signs on the hands may be too subtle for most of us to make use of or clearly perceive. But some doctors have looked at the hands for signs of breakdown for generations.

Dr. Richard Lee, a professor of medicine at the State University of New York, Buffalo, lists a number of more blatant signs showing on the hands. He says that if the hands are slightly blue, this shows problems with the circulation or lungs. Reddish palms suggest alcoholism and cirrhosis of the liver. The redness is caused by the veins enlarging. Someone who is jaundiced, who smokes, or who has a toxic condition caused by working with or taking chemicals may have a yellow tinge. This yellow color may also apply to people with high fat levels in their blood.

He also says bluish nails can be due to circulation problems or metal poisoning. Small hemorrhages under the fingernails may be "associated with circulating parasites like trichinosis [a parasite contracted by eating raw or undercooked pork] or with infections of the heart valve or in the blood vessels so that little clumps of bacteria or parasites are being shed and show up under the finger nail." Dr. Lee tells of a patient who experienced an undiagnosable fever: "The tip-off was the red streaks under her fingernails. She had trichinosis. This nice Italian lady was making her own sausage and sampling the mixture before cooking it."

If the normal curvature of the fingernails is reversed, causing a spoon shape, the subject may be deficient in iron, or it may indicate an underactive thyroid or rheumatic fever. This is different with hyperthyroidism, in which the nails grow so fast they do not adhere to the skin properly. Dr. Eugene Scheimann gives an indication of thyroid problems as dry, doughy hands and thin, brittle nails. Small, round pits in the nails suggest psoriasis. Thick, soft fingernails, looking rather like a club, can indicate lung or congenital heart disease. Someone who has recently suffered a serious illness or major surgery will probably show a "Beau's line." This is a definite groove or ridge growing across the nails, caused by a temporary stoppage in growth.

Other fingernail abnormalities include dark discolorations, which may spread to the finger tissue and signify malignant melanoma; white coloration beneath the nails, indicating cirrhosis of the liver; and nails that are half brown or pink near the tip with the other half white, indicating kidney failure.

Janet H. Silverstein, M.D., of the University of Florida College of Medicine, in researching the connection between the hands and diabetes in children, says complications are more likely to develop if the children have stiff finger joints caused by thickened connective tissue around those joints. Children with these stiffened joints have an 83 percent risk of damage to their blood vessels after sixteen years of diabetes, with a 25 percent risk if the fingers move freely. Janet Silverstein has so far not been able to discover the cause for these differences in the finger joints. Similar observation of the hands is being used to diagnose which victims of childhood diabetes are more likely to develop dangerous side effects of the illness such as eye and kidney problems.

## A Doctor Using Hand Analysis

One of the pioneers of hand analysis in medicine during our own century was Dr. Eugene Scheimann. His well-known book, *A Doctor's Guide to Better Health Through Palmistry* was published a quarter century ago.

Scheimann believes that our psychological disposition deeply influences our hands and has a great deal to do with personal health. He said in an interview, "Sure I read the lines of the hand. They tell the person's emotional state. What do I look at in the hand? Everything. If a person has a large index finger, they want to be the boss. This drive to be the boss may create hypertension or ulcers."

The more hands you look at, the more you learn about human nature and the body, and the more useful you can be to those you counsel. Hand analysis is still not a science, but a great deal can be done with it as an art. After all, one of the greatest pleasures is to have an intelligent and informed person listen to us and examine us in a sympathetic way.

# Bibliography

Altman, Nathaniel, *Sexual Palmistry* (The Aquarian Press, Wellingborough, 1986).

Benham, William G., *The Laws of Scientific Handreading* (Putnam & Co., New York, 1958).

Brandon-Jones, David, *Practical Palmistry* (Rider, London, 1981).

Dukes, Shifu Terence, *Chinese Hand Analysis* (Aquarian, London, 1988).

Fitzherbert, Andrew, *Hand Psychology* (Angus & Robertson, London and Sydney, 1986).

Gettings, Fred, *The Book of the Hand* (Paul Hamlyn, London, 1965).

Hipskind, Judith, *Palmistry, the Whole View* (Llewellyn, St. Paul, Minnesota, 1977).

Hutchinson, Beryl, *Your Life in Your Hands* (Faber & Faber Ltd., London, 1933).

Jacquin, Noel, *The Hand of Man* (Faber & Faber Ltd., London, 1933).

Jacquin, Noel, *The Hand Speaks* (Lyndoe & Faber, London, 1942).

Jacquin, Noel, *The Signature of Time* (Faber & Faber Ltd., London, 1950).

Napier, John, *Hands* (George Allen & Unwin, London, 1980).

Revesz, Gesa, *The Human Hand* (Routledge & Kegan Paul, London, 1958).

Scheimann, Eugene, *A Doctor's Guide to Better Health Through Palmistry* (Parker Publishing Co., Inc., New York, 1966).

Sen, K. C., *Hast Samudrika Shastra* (D. B. Taraporevala, Bombay, 1960).

Sorell, Walter, *The Story of the Human Hand* (The Bobbs-Merrill Co., Indianapolis, 1967).

Spier, Julius, *The Hands of Children* (Routledge & Kegan Paul, London, 1955).

Warren-Davis, Dylan, *The Hand Reveals* (Element Books Ltd., Shaftesbury, 1993).

Wolff, Charlotte, *The Human Hand* (Methuen, London, 1942).

# Index